# Atlantis Rising

The Sirian Revelations

I find myself in a cave, observer of the scene. There is an altar there. Its base is a large copper-like spiral, which stands about twelve feet high on earthen ground. Positioned upon it is a flawless crystal sphere and within this huge quartz globe is embedded a gold filament, curled in an S shape, like a snake preparing to strike.

At one point, I understand that by sending thoughts up the coppery coil, I can light up the crystal – the whole cave lights up every time I send a thought through the coil. Here I begin to channel some highly significant information about multidimensional realities, parallel universes and the true meaning of alchemy.

I entertain myself by sending these thoughts up the spiral and watching the crystal sphere light up like a street lamp! Instantly, the cave becomes completely illuminated and I see the walls lined with crystals and copper wire spirals, connected to raw emeralds. The entire structure is an intricate design of pure quartz and amethyst crystals, coppery wire spirals, emeralds, and gold filaments linking to other crystals.

I shout out from my vantage point: "I'm in the central generator room here!" and then I wake up, sweating cold… haunted by the sense that, more than just a recurring dream, this is a real memory of Atlantis, rising from the very depths of my soul.

This memory of Atlantis prompted the book cover painting by Roberta Bongiovanni

# Atlantis Rising

## The Struggle Of Darkness And Light

*Patricia Cori*

Authors Choice Press

San Jose  New York  Lincoln  Shanghai

**Atlantis Rising**
The Struggle Of Darkness And Light

Authors Choice Press
an imprint of iUniverse.com, Inc.

For information address:
iUniverse.com, Inc.
5220 S 16th, Ste. 200
Lincoln, NE 68512
www.iuniverse.com

ISBN: 0-595-20203-9

Printed in the United States of America

*To Alick Bartholomew,
my agent, editor and friend,
for his courage to reach past limitation
his vision of what lies beyond and
his dedication to bringing the light of knowledge
to the world.*

The Sirian Revelations

# Contents

# *Introduction*

My first 'conscious' connection to the Speakers of the Sirian High Council began in 1996, just weeks after strange and synchronistic events brought me into contact with the crop circle phenomenon occurring across the English countryside.

I was in England that summer to complete an advanced color therapy course at the Hygeia Institute, a renowned College for Color Healing. This was an intensive training program for color practitioners, taught from nine in the morning straight through until dinner, after which we usually studied and crammed for exams well into the late hours–so sleep was of primary importance. Fortunately, the idyllic setting of the college, the gardens and country air provided much needed peace and serenity so that, despite the disadvantages of cramped quarters and dormitory-style accommodations, I always slept like a baby, relishing every minute of rest and renewal.

One week through the course, however, I was jolted from deep sleep at four in the morning by a startlingly vivid dream in which I saw myself flying over Stonehenge, high above the lush green farmlands surrounding the monument. Gazing at the site from this aerial perspective, I was surprised to see imprinted in the neighboring field a complex spiral of graduated circles, whose dimensions increased as they unfolded from the epicenter and then, at the apex point, descended in the same proportions through to the last circle of its tail. I knew this pattern to be a perfect representation of Pythagoras's Golden Mean ratio (the sacred geometry of Earth biology) as we had just studied it in that day's lessons, and that the dream was somehow telling me that sacred geometry was meant to be an extremely important aspect of the message.

Staring down at the colossal image, I was amazed to see that this formation was almost ten times the size of Stonehenge and I wondered what it could be. A familiar voice replied that it was a 'lock-on point for extraterrestrial intelligence' and that I was to pay absolute attention…that this glyph was going to have a profound meaning for me and that it would not be long before I would understand just how profound that would be.

I woke up knowing I had received some sort of urgent cosmic communication, with not a clue as to its meaning. Excited, I recounted the dream to the other students over breakfast, and we all seemed to resonate on some level to the information that had come forth. After all, it does set the imagination buzzing–thoughts of E.T.s connecting in the dream state–and for all of us there was a buzz in the air as we left in a motor caravan for a field trip to Glastonbury. It was as if we all knew, somehow, that the message was foreshadowing of something we were going to discover there, and that the real purpose of our visit was to retrieve the information that would help me decipher the iconography of the spiral into language we could all understand.

Glastonbury being a smorgasbord for lovers of things metaphysical, the town was a natural shopper's paradise for our group, so no sooner had we arrived than we circumvented our original intention to explore the sacred sites of Avalon and headed, instead, to the Growing Needs Bookstore across the road from Glastonbury Abbey.

Upon entering the shop, my eyes instantly fell upon an exact, poster-size image of the spiral formation I'd seen in the dream, apparently photographed from a plane flying directly over Stonehenge, so that the monument was seen in direct relationship to the sculpture. Dumbfounded, I asked the cashier what the huge spiral image was supposed to represent. She told me that it was 'the latest crop circle formation', which had formed just across the road from Stonehenge. I stared incredulously at the stunning image–an absolutely perfect blueprint of my dream–knowing with absolute certainty that I had been 'called' to the crop circles, a phenomenon I had only barely heard of before that incredible date with fate…the summer of 1996.

Was I paying attention? You can be sure nothing else mattered in that moment. I discovered aerial photo shots of that summer's crop glyphs in every bookstore and notice board in Glastonbury, and there was no question that my guides had paved the way for me to experience the phenomenon first hand. Of one thing I was certain: the spiral of circles that appeared to have been blown into the wheat crop at Stonehenge held something extremely important for me and yes, I was most definitely 'tuned in'.

At that moment, I realized without a doubt that the real reason I had come to England was to learn and experience the crop circles and that the color therapy course had only been a means to that end. You just know when the universe is laying it all out for you—the master plan unfolding before your eyes. In those moments, you really understand synchronicity and know that you are in the flow of it all, feeling the exhilaration of riding the wave and trusting that where it is taking you is where you are meant to be.

Validation was everywhere around me, so it was no surprise to learn that that very evening marked the closing night of the annual crop circle conference, where the leading expert on the phenomenon, Colin Andrews, would be lecturing specifically about the Stonehenge circle.

Having shared the details of the dream with the bookstore staff, I was reassured that, although the conference had sold out months earlier, the story of my astral flight over the Julia Set would get me a seat…and it did. It just seemed that everyone in Glastonbury that summer was so completely attuned to the circle energies that it was as if we were all predestined to be there. The feeling was exhilarating and so sublime, like watching an enormous wave crash violently against the shoreline, and then following its path as it rolls back out…in the calm of the sea's unceasing rhythm.

I knew I had to be there. So, at the risk of remaining stranded there that night, I secured a seat at the lecture and then advised the others that I had decided to attend the conference, even if it would mean hitching a ride back to the college. Fortunately, the driver of my van was just as happy to spend the evening in Glastonbury, so it was agreed that the other cars would go ahead, while we would return at the conclusion of the conference. As usual, the universe provided the way, the people and the place for the appropriate connections to be made. Things do work that way when we let ourselves follow the river.

What I learned in the conference was so vast and exciting that I felt compelled to stay on in Glastonbury, forsaking the college and the color healing training. Colin Andrews, the pioneer of crop circle investigations, would be bringing a group from the conference to Stonehenge the next morning and I wanted to go, caught up in the excitement and the moment.

I knew it was important that I enter into the circle formation, to feel something there, yet my commitment and investment in the work I had undertaken at the college brought me to my senses. Somewhat begrudgingly, I joined up with the others and headed back to the Institute—my head spinning with galactic thoughts and the wonder of what new energies were manifesting in my world.

The next morning, the breakfast table was buzzing with crop circle talk, as was to be expected after such a remarkable discovery. Animatedly, we pored over the bookstore photographs of the crop circle and all agreed they were absolutely identical to what I had recounted and sketched for them just days before as 'dream material'. I shared what details of the phenomenon I had gathered from the lecture and the others were transfixed, knowing that we were opening to something fantastically exciting, and that mine was an experience meant to be shared by all.

One of the teachers was drawn into the excitement of my discovery after comparing the crop circle photos with my earlier sketch of the dream vision—as we all were. In his opinion, I was never going to have clarity to its meaning unless I physically entered the circle...yet that seemed so unlikely, given our tight schedule and the distance from the college to Stonehenge. Convinced that it was that important, he volunteered to drive me there, to facilitate an experience that we both knew had to happen. I just had hold out another week, until the course was completed...a tall order, considering my anticipation of what awaited me at Salisbury Plain.

After suffering impatiently through seven long days of classes, lectures and final exams, the course finally reached conclusion with a farewell dinner and emotional good-byes. The professor and I set off early the next morning, both of us acknowledging a feeling that something extraordinary was about to happen. Like the voice in the dream had said, the glyph held some 'profound' meaning for me. Just how profound, however, I still could not imagine.

After three long hours in the heavy traffic of weekend vacationers and map-wielding tourists, we finally approached the Neolithic stone circle of Stonehenge but, despite its awesome presence, I had no desire to stop and explore the monument. My interest in that moment lay exclusively in the surrounding field, anxious as I was to locate the crop circle. Although it was not visible from the road, Colin Andrews had given us the signs to locate the entrance into the circle, and we quickly identified the farmer's parked pick-up truck and the dirt driveway leading into the site. We were there.

The first thing that struck me about this phenomenon was how very few people were even aware of it. You would think this would be one of the most important happenings in the country! I counted no more than ten visitors moving through the field, quietly passing from circle to circle, taking great care not to disrupt the lay of the crop. It left me bewildered to think that just footsteps away from one of the greatest monuments of ancient star gazers, with its swarms of 'sightseeing' tourists, lay sculpted in the wheat this breathtaking, inexplicable design...yet hardly anyone seemed to know of its existence–or care.

It was almost as if a parallel universe had materialized before my eyes, and I was witness to both in the same moment. This, one of the most significant of all the crop glyphs ever to appear in the fields, was so complex in form and intricate in beauty that it would herald a new level of complexity in a growing phenomenon that had begun, it appeared, with a simple circle over ten years earlier. To say it took my breath away would be sheer understatement.

I needed solitude in that mystical moment...and silence. Fortunately, he understood that, so I was able to enter the sacred space with no interference or distractions, leaving me free to feel and experience the powerful vibrations that seemed to actually be pulling me in towards the center. The connection was so incredibly powerful–so immediate–that at the outer borders of the field I was already beginning to slip into altered consciousness, letting go of all expectations, all conditions and the sense of self.

I was guided to the apex–the largest of the 151 circles–and there I laid down, swimming in new vibrations and knowing this was to be a life-altering experience. Instantly, I was spinning out of body and time, yielding to the overwhelming force of increasingly high-pitched whistling sounds, which carried me to a place far, far beyond the Earth lands of the Salisbury Plain.

I have no conscious memory of that trance state other than the vivid recall of having traveled those sounds as sound itself, absolutely one with the waves, with no awareness of being in any way separate from every vibration in the universe. I can state unequivocally that it was the most significant moment of my life and **I will never forget it.**

What seemed to me a second in time Arthur later confirmed was more than one hour, yet my conscious memory holds no record whatsoever of how much time I actually laid in the circle. I had been transported beyond any former point of reference, any out-of-body experience or altered state–beyond time. There was no conscious recall of the experience and no details of where I'd been…only a total and utter departure from the Earth realm and a feeling of having somehow been 'stretched' beyond the limits–a feeling that defies definition.

The drive from Salisbury back to London was a complete fog. Nothing else seemed real or significant and all I wanted was to lie down somewhere and try to unscramble my brain. Only hours after our return back to London was I able to ground myself back in body and deal with getting onto a return flight to Rome and back to my 'normal' life.

Some weeks later, the beginnings of a new adventure into the metaphysical began, and the meaning of 'normal' in my life was redefined forever. I awoke (again at 4:00 a.m.) to a strange sound–like static running through my head–as if a radio station were being tuned in the base of my brain. Instinctively, I got up and searched every room, looking for an earthly explanation, but there was nothing unusual in the house…nothing that could explain the source of the sound. The more intense it became, the more I searched for some physical explanation, but there was nothing tangible there.

In a trance-like state, I went into my studio, switched on the Mac, and watched in amazement as my fingers began to tap out a message through the keys of the computer. A channel, it appeared, had literally been blasted open!

That was the first in a long series of early morning sessions during which I have been privileged to hear and transcribe the teachings of beings who identified themselves as the 'Speakers of the Sirian High Council'…transmissions, I was told, being beamed to me from the sixth dimension.

After one year of transcribing the clear and succinct messages of the Council, a book was born. Effortlessly, the manuscript was guided into the hands of Alick Bartholomew, then Publisher of Gateway Books, who believed in the material and, soon thereafter, *The Cosmos of Soul* was contracted for publication. I felt exhilarated, having birthed the material for the Speakers, but let down…as if completion of that effort had somehow marked an ending of my most incredible journey into the metaphysical.

To my surprise, however, the 4:00 a.m. wake-up call came again, forty-eight hours later. I was given the title and the first transmissions of this, their second work: *Atlantis Rising: The Struggle of Darkness & Light*. It, too, has been an incredible journey, a process of reaching beyond my own convictions and core beliefs and accepting, without censoring, the controversial material which you are about to read. In the process of bringing the information forward, I have opened my mind to an extraordinary universal perspective that has changed my perception in wondrous ways.

At a time when the lost continent is rising to the foreground in our consciousness, the Sirian teachings help us to integrate the knowledge of Atlantis and the fear of the Late Days…fear, they tell us, that we have held in our collective memory until now. Its message is intended to educate us to the energies at work in the final hours of the Atlantean civilization. Its intention is to explore the on-going struggle which plagues humankind and our planet, while empowering us with the truth and free will choices that are ours to claim as 21st century residents of a cosmic being about to ascend into the fourth dimension.

We are asked to utilize the information to balance the scales of darkness and light at this pivotal moment—a time that parallels the Last Generation of Atlantis—for all humanity, our Earth and the Cosmos.

This is a story. A lesson. And a warning.

It begins with a most cryptic message.

*"Yours is a specific task.*

*You, Keeper of the Crystals, have returned to the 3D theater with a specific mission. As a High Priest of Ra, you have known the power of the dark warriors and hold memory of how those of the Last Generation were involved in imprinting etheric codes and electromagnetic implants in individual morphogenetic structures, while altering vibrational frequencies in Gaian geothermal fields, serving to control the mass mind of that civilization and harness Gaian energies.*

*"You do remember the Dark Priesthood's manipulation of the elements and the havoc wreaked on Planet Earth by their abuse and wanton neglect. It is happening again—13,000 Earth years later—and you, Trydjya, are **one of many** who has returned to right the scales."*

There are great numbers of Atlanteans in body now who are opening the treasure chests of humanity's collective memory, in order to work through their experience of the devastation that occurred in the Last Generation. And yes, the human race feels fear growing within, for recall of the violence of that global cataclysm and the enslavement of the race is surfacing within you all at this time. And yes, there is again a clashing of the dark and light forces, for at this time in your progression, when you are about to move into the fourth dimension, Earth's emotional body is swinging wildly between the poles and you have come to still the pendulum…to assist in the rebirthing of Gaia.

*"You of the Light have returned to calm the waters. The time is upon you and most of you are aware that you are being stirred into action. Unfortunately, the Dolphin Beings and Great Whales are being systematically exterminated and you may no longer count on their assistance. This is of grave importance for, without their sonic weaving of the oceanic frequencies, you are finding yourselves at the mercy of Earth's angry seas.*

*"Once again, as in Atlantis, Gaia's rage is crashing upon your earthly reality with a vengeance…reminding you that human alteration of her energies has surpassed all the limits and she is, once again, forcibly taking command. The negative vibration of human abuse is like a deadly bacterial infection, and like the human auto-immune system, Gaia's self-healing emotional body is rushing into action so that it can fight off the disease.*

*"This, the replaying of the Last Generation of Atlantis, will be humanity's final conflict in the material realm. Once again you find yourselves caught in the extremes of polarity with the alchemists—the manipulators of earth energies. This is as it was intended. The forces at work in Atlantis were archetypal manifestations of Earth's polarity and you have come to find resolution of those extremes at this most crucial time of ascension throughout your solar system.*

*"The alchemists of dark intent have returned to reactivate the electromagnetic grid, while imprinting new control devices in the ethers, and this is being done to you via your technology. Now, as in the Last Generation, the people of Earth are being bombarded with subliminal sounds, codes and images, electromagnetic frequencies and other mind-controlling methodologies that you know all too well, if you will only lift off the veil and remember.*

*"The coded imprints of the dark ones were stored in human DNA as race memory, so that they could later be reactivated and used by the forces of darkness to control, once again, the masses upon your planet. It is imperative that you bring this information forward now in your own consciousness, as you send it through the heart center and out to those who can understand and transmute the coded controls into light frequencies of love.*

*"You, Trydjya, must stimulate your memory of that act if you are to help neutralize that intention. Your return to the Great Pyramid has triggered initiation, which will be completed in the subterranean chamber, where you will journey into that past lifetime…the Last Generation of Atlantis.*

*"You will be guided to see with your inner eye the story of history untold. You, Keeper of the Crystals, accessed the mindlight generators of Atlantis. You have known the cool, dark tunnels and amethyst healing caves of the inner worlds of Gaia, just as you have basked in the sunlit Chromodome of the Poseidon healing temple and the great pyramids of Atlán, where all was illuminated in the radiance of Ra, your Solar Deity.*

*Wake up now, child of Atlantis. It is time for school."*

Looking back, glimmers of buried Atlantean memories began to flutter across my mind's eye as early as age five, when (to my mother's bewilderment) I quite suddenly developed a peculiar phobia of bridges. I still vividly recall the terror of traveling with my family over the San Francisco Bay Bridge, while crossing the Golden Gate was always a scene of sheer hysteria. My mother would have to sit in the back seat with me, a blanket over my head, talking me through the trauma, until we were back on *terra firma* at the other side, and this went on well into the pre-teen years. Other than those inexplicable attacks of phobic anxiety, I was a normal, happy and well-adjusted kid, which added to the enigma of the bridge crises.

In those moments, I would feel a gripping fear that the water was going to wash over the bridge and pull me down into the bottom of the sea, as it had before...somewhere before...somewhere my child mind remembered at the primordial level. Somewhere before, in Atlantis.

There was also a persistent recurring dream, in which time and time again I would be swept off the shore of an unfamiliar beach and pulled out to sea, where I would struggle desperately underwater, trying to save myself from the deep, yet unable to recognize top from bottom as I slowly drowned. Looking back, I realize that these were truly odd dreams for a six-year-old and they persisted well into my adult years. A psychic child, my personal experiences and unexplainable insights often challenged the dogma of the day. It was a time when such things were much less accepted than they are now, in light of the age upon us. I spoke openly about Atlantis, Plato's so-called 'mythical' land, knowing my fascination with the lost continent was far more than mere curiosity. There were flashes of memory...pictures of crystal caves and sun-lit towers that returned again and again into my consciousness.

Atlantis. It was part of me, so deep within me that I had carried it through other lifetimes and into the body of a child who wept at bridges. And I would get in touch with that memory, no matter how long I would have to search for answers.

Years prior to my first clear communications from the Speakers, I had had the opportunity to work with a gifted past life regressionist in Boston who guided me on a three-hour journey through five different lifetimes. The most significant of these I experienced as Atlán, a city as modern as any we know today, with its impressive skyline of tall, glistening towers and pyramidal temples.

Guided past the distractions of the chattering mind, I soon found myself standing before an enormous crystalline pyramid, a structure that had no markings of any kind and no sign of an entrance. Yet, I knew that I could penetrate its outer wall simply by placing my hand at a certain point on the surface, because I was 'of the Priesthood'. I explained to the regressionist that we, the privileged of Atlán, held the secret codes within the left palm, allowing us entry into every temple and energy station of Atlantis.

In the next moment—like blinking into another frame—I was inside the pyramid, very aware of standing in its absolute epicenter and knowing that such a strategic position was important to my aligning with the cosmic energies there. A teacher of the Secret Wisdom, I was instructing a group of twelve initiates, all seated at ground level in the angular boundary of the pyramid's perimeters. The priests wore simple indigo-colored robes, similar in style to those of Benedictine monks, but the fabric was a brilliant, iridescent weave that held the light in such a way that it seemed to glow in the dark. Nothing like this material exists in our modern world, a consideration that seemed to hold some great clue as to why I had returned to witness this moment in my subconscious memory.

Guided to examine the scene more closely, I became aware that, more than teaching, I was actually receiving some sort of transmissions. It seemed the source was there among them, but I was having difficulty identifying it. Directed by the regressionist, I peered into the contingent of initiates to see that a woman—a luminous, penetrating figure—had risen to her feet and, with eyes that shone golden laser-like rays directly into mine, was actually performing a form of thought transference that radiated into my consciousness as 'The Wisdom'. That light, I realized, I then transmuted into language for the priests, who had come to receive the knowledge...for, as new initiates, they were still not attuned to receive the frequency directly from Source.

I was told that she was Kataar, a guide from another dimension, who had accompanied me through all my physical incarnations since my first appearance in Atlantis. It wasn't until a few years later, when I began to receive the Council's transmissions of *Cosmos*, that I realized the incredible: that not only had I been in direct contact with the Sirians as far back as then, but that this brilliant being, Kataar of the High Council, had been serving as a personal guide through these, my missions in the Earth realm.

Directed by the regressionist to examine the scene with still greater circumspection, I observed the actual energy exchange taking place in the pyramid, which appeared as a triangular configuration of golden white light moving between us. Kataar, the initiator, sent the 'cosmic wisdom' along the beams of concentrated laser light; I, the transmitter, decoded the frequencies and sent them to the priests as language; they, receivers, sent their acknowledgement to her telepathically, completing a circuit.

As I studied the scene, the energy triangulation began to multiply, folding out into a network of golden triangles–a luminous web–and we were at once surrounded by a breathtaking light show of symmetry and form. It was a golden glow reaching out into galactic infinity, a spectacular display of energy unfolding: the Gossamer Web of Light.

In the midst of it all, I became acutely aware that one of the initiates, seated in the corner off to the left off the group, had become suspiciously furtive and was, indeed, very dark–the Judas. Sensing that I had tuned into him, he slipped his hood over his eyes to escape scrutiny, trying to go undetected. As the cloak of darkness enveloped him, waves of negative energy began to permeate the space. I felt it thrust into me–an ominous, threatening force–and I knew at once that his covert presence amongst us was of the dark intention.

In the same moment that I was butted with the powerful blast of black energy, Kataar sent the message: "We have interference here...I am shutting down transmission." She called the light back in; the triangles of light began to close back down; and the regression screeched to an almost immediate halt.

The darkness beneath that hood haunted me for a long time after the session, released from the obscure depths of my subconscious and brought forward now as a piece of some yet undefined puzzle. I sensed that it was foreshadowing of an initiation that lay before me somewhere further along the path, and I knew that the cloaked intruder would manifest sooner or later, at some point down the road.

Or had it happened just that way before...shadows of a lifetime in Atlán?

*　　　*　　　*

'Keeper of the Crystals'.

That I'd been a crystal worker in an Atlantean lifetime certainly could explain my fascination with the mineral kingdom, and my years of dedication to the joyous work of healing with crystals.

My first collection consisted of chunks of quartzite and other specimens that I gathered on my own in the hills behind our house, where I used to unearth every kind of rock and stone, fossil samples, Indian arrowheads and other gifts from the fertile fields. My collection of earth things soon filled my bedroom and spilled over into the hallway. Fortunately, I was blessed with a loving and generous mother, who encouraged my childhood passion and inquisitive mind, as she does to this day.

I still recall the time she took me to a mineral shop to buy me my very first quartz crystal. We both know now that it was the call of Atlantis that brought us there—mother and child—and that it had been a far more magical moment than she had realized then: a moment that would last forever.

Looking back, I realize I was obsessed with crystals as far back as the first grade, when I was panicking over bridges and dreaming of drowning in the depths of the ocean. I would spend hours in my room, playing with the rocks and mineral I'd gathered...but I was always fascinated by the quartz point my mother had bought me. It was the pride of my collection, for it held within it a most incredible rainbow, and I would lose myself in the prisms of its light…my first conscious astral journeys. This was relatively strange behavior in 1958, well before the rage of crystalmania had become the fashion of the day, and certainly not a typical distraction for a six-year-old. I can remember so clearly gazing long hours into that brilliant quartz point, traveling the bridge of its rainbow, just as a ray of light pours through the windowpane of a darkened room.

What my mother dismissed as 'daydreaming' was actually a child retrieving skills and memories of other lifetimes. Unknown to either of us at the time, that generator crystal was re-activating within me my connection to Atlantis, although it would take another forty years before I would finally unveil the memory and recover the experience of the Last Generation. Only then would I finally remember the purpose of my reincarnating now, in the final confrontation between the light and dark forces—a prelude to the transmutation of Gaia.

For a time, I put aside the crystal teachers, too busy growing up and getting through puberty to discover any other lives but this. As is usually the way with psychic children, the awareness and vision of my early childhood years waned, giving way to the emotional roller coaster of life as a budding young woman: needing to be nurtured; dealing with sex; falling in and out and back in love; and traveling half way around the world before the Atlantis 'dreams' began.

Like the pages of a novel, my dreams wove a fantastic tapestry of richly colored landscapes, reflections of a subconscious filled with crystalline grottoes and turquoise seas, forests clustered in emeralds and quartzes the size of trees, translucent pyramids and great flying ships, which moved me through the scenes of my mind. There have been fantastic images of crystal towers, healing chambers and solar engines, and always I know I am remembering a land I have loved and wept and celebrated as my true home.

One recurring dream has dominated the fields of my sleeping mind for so long that I can barely remember when it first began its haunting reappearance in the dreamtime. It is always exactly the same...never altering. Now, after so many encounters with the memory, every detail is indelibly etched in my mind.

*I find myself in a cave, observer of the scene. There is an altar there. Its base is a large copper-like spiral, which stands about twelve feet high on earthen ground. Positioned upon it is a flawless crystal sphere, and within this huge quartz globe is embedded a gold filament, curled in an S shape, like a snake preparing to strike.*

*Observing this altar is a young boy, about ten or twelve years old, dressed in amethyst robes. He wears golden serpents coiled around the neck and wrists. There is an aristocracy and intensity about him way beyond his years, and he exudes an air of ageless confidence. It is a commanding presence.*

*Standing next to him is a woman—a priestess—dressed in a gown of luminescent white 'mother of pearl', which seems to bounce light off its every curve and border.*

*I am only watching, though; I am not a participant in the actual scene. The priestess is teaching the boy about energy and its manifestation. He is the overseer of the generators, the Keeper of the Energy.*

*At one point, I understand that by sending thoughts up the coppery coil, I can light up the crystal—the whole cave lights up every time I send a thought through the coil. Here I begin to channel some highly significant information about multidimensional consciousness, parallel universes and the true meaning of alchemy, which I realize is coming through to the dream from guidance. I am experiencing how thought is light...that thought creates light...that light is thought in its crystalline expression.*

*I feel such exhilaration in this dream! I am being shown how totally simple it all is...as if 'simplicity', of itself, were a big awakening. I begin to entertain myself by sending these thoughts up the spiral and watching the crystal sphere light up like a street lamp! Instantly, the cave becomes completely illuminated and I can see that the walls are lined with crystals and copper wire spirals, connected to bits of raw emeralds. The entire structure is an intricate design of pure quartz and amethyst crystals, coppery wire spirals, emeralds, and gold filaments linking to other crystals.*

*I shout out from my vantage point: "I'm in the central generator room here", and then I wake up, sweating cold...haunted by the sense that, more than just a recurring dream, this is a real memory of Atlantis, rising from the very depths of my soul.*

# Chapter 1

## The First Transmissions

A contemporary understanding of personal evolution–your acceleration into fully conscious 21st century human beings–requires profound introspection, commitment, and integration of the logical and intuitive halves of the mind. It entails a clearing of old programming, release of blocked energy forms, and a new approach to living as caretakers of the celestial being upon whom you reside and take nourishment. Involved is the full awakening of the heart and the silencing of the ego-driven self. These are the fundamental processes that will determine how you will approach the process of planetary transformation, while defining your personal experience of ascension from the realm of matter.

As you move ever closer to the fated date of the closing Mayan calendar (December 21, 2012), you are becoming increasingly alarmed over the prospect of an impending global disaster–the Armageddon scenario–which has been rendered a highly possible reality through senseless nuclear proliferation, your poisonous waste and your rage. Indeed, manifestations of upheaval have already begun at every corner of the world. Perhaps, many fear, it is too late…and you are careening towards the inevitable, with no way to break your fall. Others understand how you create your realities with every thought, every word and gesture…that it can be a smooth ride if you focus upon 'right action'–your minds centered, clear and filled with wonder over your potential as the New Aquarians of Planet Earth.

It is at the same time frightening, yet exciting, for you know, on some intuitive level, that you have experienced this before. Humanity obviously survived. As reincarnating beings, you have known death and rebirth over and over again, although most of you do not consciously remember your passage in and out of the physical realm. But this is quite different. Those who have opted to be born into this Earth era are experiencing the death, or transmutation, of the entire planet, and you are in the thick of it, holding on for dear life, your happiness and security constantly threatened by the specter of total annihilation.

Like the people of late Atlantis, you seem to be on the brink, anticipating your plunge into the abyss. Your concept of life and of your purpose as human beings is changing; your fragility and impermanence are ever more present in your minds; your greater home, the very earth beneath your feet, is in 'clear and present' danger.

It is a difficult but challenging time and, therefore, you would do well to remember, no matter how your personal circumstances may otherwise appear, that you have **chosen** to be here.

Although it may seem incomprehensible to you at the conscious level, you do know about planetary evolution…the transmutation of form and biological systems. Humanity has experienced it before, when the great antediluvian civilization of Atlantis reached such a state of disharmony that it short-circuited the energy networks of the planet, and life was nearly obliterated at many corners of the Earth.

The power structure of the time (the omnipotent forces of the Dark Priesthood of Atlán) believed, in their blind arrogance, that they could own even the forces of Gaia, harnessing her like a beast of burden. They pushed beyond the limits, and all was virtually washed away in the Great Flood, as Gaia cleansed her body of the intense negative vibration and brought herself back to center to start again, renewed and revitalized.

Here you are, once again, setting the Goddess off course, throwing everything out of balance in your exacerbation of the duality that underlies three-dimensional reality. From your limited vantage point, it appears that the very nature of existence is based on the war between good and evil and even now, as you spiral into the future, you are faced with this dualism at every juncture…in every moment of your lives. You may have resigned yourselves to the idea that there is no hope for humanity–that you have reached the point of no return–and **that is a dangerous, self-defeating belief structure.** It only feeds the darkness, empowering those who believe they own you to take more from you. It amplifies the darkness, catapulting you even further into despair. It takes your light…your power…your joy.

You live in a world which hosts both extremely dark characters and wondrously loving, spiritual beings, but the truth is that most of humanity is somewhere in-between. Each of you knows and has confronted the brilliance as well as the shadow of your own persona, and that is the duality–the very nature of life as you know it in the human experience. There have been moments of incredible radiance and impenetrable darkness throughout history and these two extremes, you find, often exist in the same moment, occupying the same space as poles of the one energy. The poles clash and conflict with each other and yet, you realize, they are simply reflections of the whole.

As students of esoteric wisdom, you are learning that you must integrate the polar aspects: the good and bad; the light and dark; the love and hate. As long as you continue to fuel these forces in opposition, there will be war on every level.

Now, more than ever, the fighting and conflagrations surround you, and humanity seems lost in the senselessness of violence and despair. It is a time of extremes in behavior, when these aspects have, once again, come into absolute conflict. Human suffering, the disregard for life and beauty, and the abuse of those who seek power over others seem to have become the overriding experience of your contemporary civilization, causing you to question just how much it is that the human race has actually progressed in its course of social evolution.

You are reliving, at this time in history, the same undercurrents, energy manipulation and abuse of power that exemplified the last generations of Atlantis...a civilization that had reached (in some aspects) a much higher level of technological prowess than that which you know today. It was a society that enjoyed direct assistance from multidimensional beings who trained and worked with the Priesthood (themselves descendants of other realms). Their enhanced capabilities and understanding of the universal laws and elemental forces qualified them as Keepers of the Records.

These gifts of extraterrestrial knowledge were intended to raise the consciousness of your ancestors, bringing them a sense of their part in the greater scheme of things. Paradoxically, the priestesses of the early generations used the Wisdom for the light while, goaded by the Annunaki, later generations of the Priesthood saw some of the Brotherhood swing to the dark side, turning their acquired knowledge–their gifts–against the people. How can you help but notice that the time of darkness, the flagrant abuse of the Wisdom, is happening again?

We, Speakers of the Sirian High Council, confirm that many of the sophisticated technologies resulting from that exchange are being utilized against humanity and against Gaia. In their all-consuming pursuit of power, the dark priests of Atlán, united with others of Annunaki lineage, have reincarnated now. We assure you that they are more ravenous than ever in their hunger to harvest and consume your energy, your power and your resources. Could it be that you are going to have to relive the fall of Atlantis all over again?

It is a devastating alliance, that of the dark force, yet **the light is all around you.** You have only to set your intention, your group mind, to penetrate and disarm the perpetrators of ignorance. Know that, no matter how determined others might be to draw upon your power, darkness can only feed on darkness and that, we remind you, is nothing more than fear, ignorance and rage. By remembering the structural nature of the dark pole, you can move through the coming Earth Changes without suffering and pain. It is your choice to make...it always has been.

You can still alter the outcome so that, this time, the manipulation of energy and the abuse of power occurring in your realm will not have to result in the devastation that once before erased almost all life from the Great Planet Earth. You can choose not to suffer in any way whatsoever the coming transformation; rather, you can anticipate with eagerness the process of re-birthing your planet, honoring your soul's intention to take part in that experience.

But will you? Will you, children of Atlantis? Or will you tell yourselves that it is impossible that the human hand could have so drastically changed the course of an entire planet, and that *Atlantis Rising* is just a story…a grown-up's fairy tale, of which there exists no tangible proof or evidence? By removing all record of Atlantis from you, rendering 100,000 years of a continent's prominence upon the face of the Earth a mere legend, the power elite has, until recently, succeeded in concealing from you the greatest plundering of life and resources ever to occur in your world.

We suggest that if you prefer to receive these teachings as fiction—if doing so will allow your logical minds to read on where otherwise you might dismiss the information as pure fantasy—then we are happy to serve you as simple storytellers. Or, you may wish to consider our material a key to unlocking your own Atlantean memories, reassured in the realization that we are not asking you to discard all other beliefs and writings regarding the true history of humankind.

We are not so assuming or ego-centered as to interfere with your personal experience, whereby you acquire at your own pace the knowledge of what human experience preceded yours. Nor would we disturb your free will fields of vision by dogmatically spelling out an irreversible future in some prophetic verse from the stars, for you have had enough of the seers and their predictions to know that **you are constantly changing the outcome of your reality.**

One assumption that can be made, however, is that if you have been drawn to these teachings it is no doubt because, like our instrument, you were there…one of the Last Generation of Atlantis.

And here you are again, at the edge of reality, beginning to remember.

As you brush away the cobwebs and peer down the hallways of your minds, you painstakingly gather the bits of memory, faded tiles of an ancient mosaic, re-creating images of what you consider your 'past'. There are holes, places where the images fade, and it is here that we wish to help you fill in the missing pieces.

It is our intention to provide the lost information–the guarded Atlantean secrets–that will challenge you to reclaim the power and establish your freedom, stimulating you into seeking the truths that for so long have lain hidden below the shifting sands of time.

Truth or fantasy? You, Atlanteans of the new Earth millennium, are re-writing the future from the tattered manuscripts of your buried memories and you hold the answer to that question **within you**.

Dare to gaze deep down inside the well and you will see Truth's gentle ripple in your souls…ever so subtle, like a soft breeze on still waters.

# Chapter 2

## Atlantis Rises

*"You are remembering Atlantis at this time because you must now expand your vision to include possible realities that you have ignored or forgotten."*

—*The Cosmos of Soul*

Atlantis has been the subject of much speculation, research and fantasy, for the lost continent lies buried in your group mind–your universal memory–and at a time when modern Earth society parallels the Atlantean model, you are pulling it up into consciousness, rediscovering your ancestral selves. As humanity exacerbates the technological advancement of these, the late years of Gaia, you are beginning to identify, in the tales of Atlantis, the archetypal energies and geo-thermal forces that are shaking you from your beds and forcing you to confront the future as 21ˢᵗ century residents of what **appears** to you to be a rapidly dying planet.

Information alluding to the abuse of power and technology in the Last Generation has begun to surface in your group consciousness, enabling you to realize more succinctly how the destruction of Atlantis parallels your present situation. Still, most of your research and artistic expression reflects a glorification of the High Culture of that civilization, for the memory of the late days is too painful and frightening, which is why you have buried it deep in the subconscious–silent testimony of a deliberately forgotten past.

Yet, you need it. You, the human race, need to shine the light into the dark corners of your memory, so that you can recognize the Atlantean paradigm at this time in your planet's evolutionary journey. The ancient lesson serves you now. It is our intention to assist you in first retrieving and then processing the experience that lies dormant within you. By stimulating the recall of that enormous struggle–the clashing of the forces of dark and light in the late hours of Atlantis–we feel we may be triggering you to affect a form of group thought/behavior modification that will assist conscious human beings in altering the severity of the approaching Desert Days.

The emergency on Earth is all-encompassing, as she shakes and thunders from the depths of her inner being, preparing you for an inevitable passage through the storm of planetary transformation. Like the sinking of the continent of Atlantis and the ensuing deluge, the difficult process of purification–Gaia's uncontrollable response to man's abuse of power–is once again an imminent reality. You, the whole of humanity, are very much a part of the cause and effect, the symptom and the cure. All is interrelated in the cosmic dance of karmic process.

Despite your myths and mystification of a superior Atlantean culture, life was far from idyllic in the later generations, when the focus shifted from a deeply spiritual awareness to the pursuit of materialism and might, and the polarity of energies reached the extremes. Intervention from forces beyond the Earth deliberately stimulated in certain individuals behaviors that further separated the society; this we will elaborate for you in the course of these transmissions. You may even remember, for many of you were there…holding your side of the pole with conviction, working for the darkness or the light.

In that late hour of the ancient civilization's decline, the masses were enslaved–on their knees to the hierarchy–living out their victim consciousness, as they are now. Like our instrument, you may have returned to right the scales and assist those who, this time, intend to rise from their servitude and stand against the dark masters.

First, however, you must confront the shadow within you. If you are to transform those energies into the exalted fire of true power and pull the pendulum back to center, absolute concentration–your focused intent–will be essential. Gaia is calling you to action and all who can hear are shifting into position.

Much of your fascination with Atlantis is stimulated by that dichotomy, the conflicting energies of polar opposition, for with the sunken continent are buried some of the greatest and darkest hours of humanity. It is happening again–a perfect replay–and once again you are confronting yourselves: the power struggle; a misguided materialism; your fear of the future; anguish over the decaying societies of your modern world.

As is the cyclical nature of all existence, civilization has once again reached a level of development that is imploding upon itself, as excessive technology turns you into robots and you lose yourselves to the almighty mechanical god. It is stripping you of your natural intelligence, your desire and will, undermining your energetic interaction and personal exchange. Most significantly, the technology hysteria that is now overtaking human culture distorts your understanding of evolution and your purpose as individual units of consciousness of the Gaian vibration.

You have come full circle, replaying the scenes of the Last Generation of Atlantis, where humankind, driven from the sacred to the profane, was robbed of its natural place in the Great Family of Light to become the alienated of Earth. The *wam*, Earth's golden chord, that once played sweet the music of the men, women and children of Atlantis, was eventually lost to the strident march of 'progress', forcing the later generations to walk to the imperial rhythm of the master.

Prototype of current westernized Earth cultures, the Last Generation was confronted with the destructive force of its technology, which became the controlling weapon of the power elite. The Priesthood, Keepers of the Sirian records of universal mind, frequency and cosmometry, eventually succumbed to the extreme polarity of Earth's fields. Those who chose the dark side were fueled by aggressive extra-planetary entities to take power, and those same energies are ever-present in the theater of life upon your planet.

To feed the hunger of the few, the glory of one of the most expansive civilizations in Earth's history was washed up in the waves in a moment…the blinking of an eye. With it, most of the living creatures that colored your plains and highlands were either swept away in raging seas, or immortalized in the deep freeze of higher ground, where the snows pounded down upon them, obliterating their very existence. Frozen in the no-time, beings from ancient worlds are, as such, frozen in your memory and now, in the heat of the approaching Desert Days, they are soon to spring to life. With them, total recall of the Late Days will surface in the minds of those who once fought so desperately to forget.

Yet, you are here. You have overcome your terror and evolved to face this, the Great Initiation, by sheer determination, for yours is a soul quest and a commitment to the light.

Children of Atlantis, we commend you. You are the brave pioneers of humankind's true emergence and we know what strength and vision are required of you as you face the long journey.

*          *          *

Now, as you feel the walls closing in on you, the Earth shrinking and giving out under the weight of uncontrollable overpopulation and its unrelenting demands upon her, your civilization mistakenly looks to technology as a way out of the dilemma in which it finds itself. You urgently need more space, more food, water and resources. Most believe that the solutions will be reached through technology, for the greater body of Earth beings is forever giving power over to it. The almighty computer, rudimentary grandchild of Atlantean crystal mindlight generators, has momentarily distracted the population from all that is disharmonious around you, while pulling you into a false sense of resolution for a future that simply isn't there...not, at least, as you envision it.

Earth's power elite encourage your dependency upon the viewing screens of your computers and televisions, for these are the operative control mechanisms of your times. Like the Dark Priesthood of Atlán, they are turning the knowledge against you to feed their hunger, while ever-growing numbers of human beings still sit there, resigned to their impotence, playing inane games of holographic 'communication'.

And the children...what of them? They are abandoning play and discovery, laughter and innocence, their delicate minds anxiously clutching at electronic distractions. It is a travesty to observe humanity once again shutting down to true communication, which you have all but forgotten was once a great exchange of emotion, intellect and spirit between you.

**It seems that all too many human beings have lost the music, the vision and the light to the buzz, the picture and the glare.**

\*      \*      \*

If now we bring you the story of dark Atlantis, it is not because we wish to glorify or focus upon that which is the lower vibration of your past or future (as you understand time to be confinable in those terms). Rather, we wish to shake you from your illusion and show you how disempowering thoughts manifest when you allow yourselves to become victims of your own creation. We call you to reclaim your power by consciously understanding not only how it has been taken from you, but also how you continually give it away. Only then will you be prepared to recognize the instruments of control and liberate yourselves from them, so that you may participate as free beings in the Great Transformation, which is about to revolutionize forever life on your planet and throughout your solar system.

Many of you were born with shimmerings of previous life experiences and are now bringing them to full light. Others have worked to develop the faculty of past life recall and are remembering the ancient civilization of Atlantis, whose mystique has long been the inspiration of superb works of art, architecture and literature. We are aware of countless beings who are currently capitalizing on its renewed popularity to empower themselves, so be discerning, always searching within you for the intuitive response, which you know as the 'gut reaction'. These, our transmissions, are no exception. We encourage you to question all hypothetical and supposedly scientific information and find the answers…the validation…from deep within you—for it is **there** that truth is heard, once you silence yourselves enough to recognize the voice of your souls.

From the contested writings of Plato, whose *Dialogues* record tales of Atlantis as told to him by Solon, sage of Hellas, to the crystalline visions of the seer Edgar Cayce, consciousness of the lost continent has hovered somewhere between fantasy and reality for much of your recorded history. For centuries, the curious have been exploring the scientific possibilities of an entire continent being buried in the waters of the Atlantic Ocean.

That search, the lingering desire to discover your antediluvian ancestry, has facilitated many in the retrieval of the Wisdom…the 'knowing' which lies within us all. Others (those of the scientific approach) believe they must first locate the artifacts and monuments buried below the sands of the great ocean before claims of Atlantis as an irrefutable reality can be substantiated. Indeed, you are uncovering some of the proof, but you have so far to go before you can piece together the story of stories. It is a journey of self-discovery, the probing of your subconscious, where memory holds the clearest pictures and all truths lie waiting the unveiling.

As we asserted in *The Cosmos of Soul,* the continent did indeed exist in three-dimensional reality. We hear the debate amongst you as to the plane of existence of this land and we confirm to you that the concept of Atlantis as a paradigm of multidimensional consciousness—an etheric civilization—is only valid if it also acknowledges the island's physical existence on your planet. This is entirely relevant to your current situation.

During its 100,000 years of evolution, Atlantis rose and fell from greatness in three distinct cycles, knowing in its transformation the cold of barren icelands, as well as the warmth of tropical breezes. In each period, the natives achieved highly sophisticated standards of civilization and then, completing a cycle, fell into irreconcilable social decline. None, however, was more significant than the last civilization of Atlantis, which spanned a period of time dating from 27,000 to 10,800 BC, when it met with its tragic end.

In the final stages–the pre-flood years–this people demonstrated unimaginable technological prowess, and you identify with this process. You **are** the process. You, the human race, are moving your 'primitive' tools through the boundless freedom of nature into the cages of technology and cultural 'sophistication'.

In so doing, you are losing your ability to hear, to see and to sense the world around you. Like your Atlantean ancestors, you have become lazy and bored with things that do not artificially light up and lure you into new illusions–the virtual realities–for you are becoming too drugged to stand up for yourselves and find your own way. You have, once again, lost the wam vibration to the sound mechanics of your devices, and yet you still do not hear the noise of your own inventions. How, then, will you recognize the music of your souls?

In these, the late days of your generation, humanity is committing the universal error of playing God with life–the manipulation of DNA and the unlimited applications of biogenetics. This is the greatest mistake of any technologically advancing civilization. Yes, we are all co-creators, but we overshoot the mark when we envision ourselves, individual units of consciousness, capable of performing the supreme works of Prime Creator. This is effrontery to the Divine. We know...we, too, have interfered, albeit with the highest intentions, in the regenerative process of humankind's development upon Planet Earth, and that is karma we are still working to resolve.

Mutations of man and animals, the scientists' latest monstrosities, already exist in the underground, from as far back as the last generations of Atlantis, and your karmic debt is mounting. We will speak in detail of the underground of your world and the life forms that inhabit its caves and tunnels in later passages. If you believe inter-terrestrial life too preposterous to be considered a possible reality, we ask that you consider this: just exactly what do you think the mad scientists are up to there, in your underground 'biological research' centers and military installations?

Soon the mutant strains from their hidden genetics laboratories will advance on your world, and these genetically altered life forms—the complex viruses, hybrid freaks and clones—will create incredible disturbance in the natural life sequence of animals and human beings across the surface of your globe. Actually, it has already begun. You have already been exposed to a few of their hybrid creations: some of these, such as the *Chupacabras* reported in Puerto Rico and in Chile, have been causing disruption at the surface and terrorizing the locals. Others are escaping into the outer worlds of other lands and are, as yet, relatively unknown to the populace.

AIDS and other deadly super viruses are created underground and brought up to the surface, when it is deemed time for certain strains to be tested. Some have already passed the tests and are being secretly utilized in biological weapons and released upon targeted populations in the secret war that is being waged against humankind. Many more are on the way. Much more is going to be coming up from the below of your Earth in the Desert Days.

Do you still believe that 'what you do not know will not hurt you'? Do you trust that 'a little bit of knowledge can be a dangerous thing'? These are controlling thought patterns created to hold you in ignorance, and they have proven throughout history to be effective, since, paradoxically, many of your societies have embraced such expressions as 'wisdom'. We suggest that it is what you do know, the light of knowledge, that frees you and we invite you to eliminate the negative thought implants of such colloquialisms from your programming. Your fearlessness lies in your ability to trust that **knowledge is your liberation.**

Once again, as in the case of the Last Generation of Atlantis, earthquakes, continental shifts and eruptions are shattering your realities and your limited knowledge of cosmic forces makes you fear more than ever for the future of your planet and the very prospects of humanity's survival. And yet, history has shown you that violent shifts in Gaia's land masses and her polar orientations, devastating floods, fires and famines are all a reflection of Earth's infinite cycles of transmutation of form and energy in the physical realm in which she has existed until now.

Know that life cannot be annihilated, for within the consciousness of every living thing–every cell, molecule and atom–is the seed thought of Supreme Being, the Primal Will, which knows no other purpose than to Be. And so, life mutates and evolves, but never does the soul cease to exist, for all is in an eternal state of 'becoming' in the Universe.

Observe. Through a crack in the pavement, a blade of grass grows, having found its way around the impenetrable barrier and into the warmth of the Sun. Life forever pushes forward, always moving toward the light, always seeking illumination. That is simply the nature of the expanding consciousness of All-That-Is. Even those who choose to linger in the shadows of darkness will eventually move beyond them, for inherent in the meaning of the All is the leaving and the returning of every conscious being to the absolute light of Prime Creator.

Fear not for the future of humanity. Once again, you will stand face-to-face with the fury of Gaia's revolt, but you can determine to what degree that energy explodes around and within you. We do not deny that many will be lost from your world, passing into other states of being or reincarnating on another planet body. As difficult as it is for you to believe, those are decisions that were made long before they passed through the birth canal of the mother and entered physical form as Earth residents.

At the soul level, they are at peace with that probable outcome. At the conscious level, understandably, there can be much fear and suffering, which is why we have come to help you through the passing. We are searching for ways to bring you through without pain and despair, while holding in our awareness the laws of non-interventionism. It is no simple task.

Slowly, the mass mind is awakening to the fact that your planet has entered a phase of quite drastic geophysical disturbance, while you sit at the edge of time, watching your beliefs being uprooted like trees in the hurricane. Look around you. Every day signals new extremes in the climate, and what are erroneously termed 'natural calamities' are occurring with ferocious frequency at every point of your globe.

Gaia's auric field, the ozone, is literally ripping apart. Without that protection, Earth cannot sustain life (as you know it) on the surface. Even the most temperate zones have begun to experience violent upheaval, as Gaia shudders and quakes beneath you, storming and pouring her rebellion down upon you.

Many are seeking the Messiahs' messages, anxious to build their survival shelters until the storm blows over. Know that there is only one safe harbor...that center of your being, where all is in balance and fear cannot take hold. Your primary task is to understand the calming of the pendulum, the next is to still your emotional bodies and **be there**. That, dear ones, is the true Ark...it is your only guarantee of safe passage into the next dimension.

We are moved by the waves of humankind's desperation and diminishing will and we wish to assist you, yet we have been shown the boundary lines. Crossing them involves interfering in your karmic process, and we have learned that lesson. We can share our insights with you and show you the road to the Wisdom, but you are the evolutionary drivers of your own destiny.

If you see destruction all around you and fear the future, it is because you have yet to understand the driving life force of death. But if you can expand your vision to reach beyond the physical signs of disruption and the catastrophes that are occurring now, you will recognize the universal truth underlying all life: that all things are in a constant state of change and that evolution, the higher reflection of that process, is cyclical.

You look at your world in despair, for there is incredible disharmony on various levels, and many believe that the end of all life is near...simply because you have digressed to a point of what seems irreconcilable social and ecological decline. That is a wrong conclusion. Humanity rises and falls like the waves of the oceans, for that is the nature of existence throughout the material universe. All things have their springtime, the newness of their days; their summer, when the most directed energies are at work; fall, when life begins to slow and wane; winter, a time of rest and preparation. And yes, you are now approaching the Gaian winter, the Desert Days of your civilization, when the ground cracks and swells with the first freeze and all seems desolate and unrelenting and then, the thaw...when the first buds of new life appear across the landscape.

The old births the new and then returns unto itself, just as from the seed unfolds the tree, which then to seed returns...and life continues.

Atlantis Rises.

# Chapter 3

## History Untold

What of the greatness of Atlantis?

You have a romanticized idea of this land and its inhabitants, your ancestors, for what little has been written or passed down from the story-tellers is a conflicting conundrum of fact and fantasy. As you begin to accept the possibility that evolved cultures pre-date your established records by tens of thousands of years, you cannot help but consider the existence of great civilizations, which prospered and passed into oblivion in the process of Earth's continual revolution. In many ways, you believe modern Earth society to be the exaltation of human potential, largely because you have such limited information and ambiguous reference of all that passed before your written record. You would be quite humbled if you could reach into the great libraries and retrieve the real story of your ancestral accomplishments, which far surpasses those of your contemporary societies.

Indeed, the story of the human being is one that rings through many galaxies, for you are unique in so many truly wondrous ways–just as you are one and the same as all life in the Cosmos. You are the creation of master geneticists from neighboring star systems and extra-dimensional realities. And, as seed of some of the most ancient civilizations in the Cosmos, you are old...much, much older than you can ever imagine.

Worshippers of technology, you identify as 'primitive' humanity as it existed before the Industrial Age...and that is ironic. Yours is an extremely limited awareness of the human journey: the peaks and valleys of civilizations that have flourished and disappeared upon the Earth for thousands of years before the last millennia of your modern times. Those great libraries–where the secrets of antediluvian record were held–have been consistently sacked and burned throughout man's passing, leaving almost no written clues to your enigmatic past. That has been deliberate. The Dark Ages of the Crusades and other moments of religious zeal and despotism saw the mass burning of your greatest wealth as a means of guaranteeing the perennial ignorance of those who would be conquered and brought to their knees.

Knowledge, the light of consciousness, empowers; ignorance, the absence of that light, enslaves. The loss of knowledge, of the wisdom of the ancients, is the greatest travesty perpetrated upon humanity, and it continues to plague you in the form of censorship, persecution and denial on many levels. It is no wonder that those of you who have the ability to access the Akashic Record have had to conceal yourselves to avoid discrimination, or mask the Wisdom in codes and riddles that would deter all but the most diligent novitiates.

Yet, proof of Atlantis lies everywhere around you. It is woven into the fabric of your ancient temples, left in effigy of enlightened civilizations whose knowledge reached the furthest points of your planet. You can find it in the tales of the Elders, who have handed down the story from generation to generation...guardedly sharing the Secret Wisdom with those who could hear it. It is in the song of nature...the rocks and crystals of Gaia, for they hold the vibrations of all that which has passed upon the face of the Earth. It is carved into the landscape, lying upon the sea bed, and coded to the stars above you. Moreover, it is stored within your DNA, lying deep within the wells of your subconscious memory.

In the brief period believed to be your history, of which you have recorded significant bits and pieces of some six thousand years of socio-anthropological process, you have observed humanity as well as the other species experience various phases of evolution. You have seen war and peace, death and renaissance, famine and abundance occurring over and over again—as life cycles of Planet Earth. And yet, the record is so very limited, for the mainstream historians have predominantly focused on the theater of aggressors and the taken…the emperors and the slaves.

History often glorifies the Power—the oppressors—those who have burned the manuscripts of knowledge, silenced the speakers of mystical truths and rearranged the pictures of the past to ensure their hold over you, while setting the vibratory tenor of life on Earth.

Never forget that it is that very power that chronicles most of the events in recorded history, and know that much has been manipulated in the telling. Your contemporary societies are still governed by these rulers, the power elite, and they continue to program your beliefs to exalt their omnipotence and hold you in obedience.

You, of the 'democratic' nations, believe you are free men and women, proud of your governmental decrees and your sacred rights and liberties. You believe in such idealistic constructs and are prepared to die to protect them. You are encouraged and taught to believe in the Patria—the ideal—which places your country above all others, and it is for this that wars and interventions are supposed to be fought in the fields of the dying. You believe in your exoteric religions, separate and unyielding, and here again your youth are sent against each other to kill any other belief but yours, always in the name of the one-and-only Divinity.

Are you so sure that yours is true liberation? Yes, you are given some harmless freedoms and not all of the Power's messages are **overtly** controlling. Do not underestimate, however, the subtle manipulation that is being perpetrated upon you at levels that are beyond human perception. Simply because your cages are masked to the physical eye does not mean you are free to run.

You have been allowed to toy with extraterrestrial visions as science fiction, yet our fields of fractal artistry and sacred geometry (the crop circles) are still dismissed as hoaxes, due to the slanted journalism of controlled media and the expert work of the new 'pranksters'. You are permitted access to the mystical temples of the ancients, yet the multidimensional energies and Secret Wisdom encoded there are dogmatically explained away in limiting three-dimensional terminology. The classicists refuse to yield to the brilliance of your new pioneers, the astro-archeologists who have begun to decipher and bring to you the magic of their Atlantean heritage…gifts of Sirian and Pleiadian legacy. Masters and slaves, conquistadors and primitives—the story is self-fulfilling and self-perpetuating.

It is knowledge, the light that they would keep from you, that empowers. That is why it is so crucial that you circumvent the dogma of convention and discover the messages left by the Wise Ones, for there are many keys available now for the seekers.

It is time you recognize your planet as a deity, for Gaia is, indeed, a celestial being and she thinks, she feels and aspires in ways that are similar to your own thoughts, emotions and dreams. The time has come for you to explore the spirit body of the Universe and look to the stars in ways that surpass the scientific probes of the Secret Government—those modern architects of power. They know so much more than they tell you of the mechanics of your universe, the beings and movement of other systems, other dimensions and worlds, and this knowledge, enhanced by your esoteric understanding—the view of the ancients—is relevant to your current situation on Planet Earth. By becoming aware of the Universe of which you are so vitally a part, you will soon recognize that the power elite are now attempting to rewrite the 'future', concealed in their glorification of a renewed thrust into space. Flags are waving once again, as they allude to the promises of new frontiers beyond the confines of Earth.

Are you alert, Earth children? Have you learned to read between the lines? Your galactic family is uniting now to bring you the information in order to rekindle the knowing that is already yours, since the days of Atlantis and well beyond…indeed, from the time of your seeding, when you held twelve strands of DNA. Representatives from many dimensions and star systems, members of the Galactic Federation, are working with the human race via frequencies that can be received by those who are attuned for that purpose, and your numbers are increasingly **dramatically**.

We are meeting more of you in the crop fields, drawing the designs of universal intelligence upon your 3D landscape. As you approach the Mayan deadline of 2012, a great number of Earth beings will be in resonance–you have that to look forward to. It is essential to your understanding of the dynamics of change that are sweeping your world, and their repercussion in the Universe.

Looking through the scant and often misinterpreted records of your last six thousand years, one encounters Gaia as a once-virgin territory where few human beings populated a limitless, luxuriant garden…where animals painted your canvass with every imaginable color of the Creator's palette. Despite the warriors and crusading moralists, whose cacophonous imprint seems burned into every epoch of human civilization, there have undoubtedly been times of greater global harmony and peaceful co-existence on Planet Earth.

Many believe that it is only in the last very few years–a mere skip of a heartbeat–that humankind, merely an aspect of the greater consciousness of Gaia, has destroyed the delicate balance. Yet, you are relatively unaware that what is occurring now on your planet is a repetition of human history–history that you have only minimally explored and which, by nature of its obscurity, has been ignored or relegated to fantasy.

Indeed, an entire continent simply disappearing from the face of the Earth! It is understandable that you have difficulty accepting that hypothesis when, in your recorded memory, there has been no such shifting of sands. Yet, your world is constantly sinking, rising and reforming itself…for Earth is a live, conscious being. You, who cling to material reality for security and the existential reason of your lives, have not understood that all beings throughout the Universe are constantly being transformed into new forms and new realities. From a minute grain of sand to the greatest star in the heavens, all is in a state of perpetual evolution.

The story of Atlantis is long and tedious, for this great culture dates back just about 100,000 Earth years, with the first appearance of *Homo Sapiens* upon your planet. Imagine…100,000 years in which entire civilizations have come and gone from the face of the Earth in a cyclical passage through time. It strains your imagination to visualize a world without electric lights (a mere century ago), so how are you to contemplate as the 'true' history of humankind 100,000 years of growth and destruction, evolution and decline?

Your search for proof of this all-encompassing reality yields so little. Not even the discovery of submerged Atlantean archeology (the Bimini Road) in the waters of the Caribbean Sea has received acknowledgement from scientists and scholars. Despite the indisputable perfection of design–the intelligence evidenced in the formation of the stones–the road is still dismissed by the mainstream as an 'unexplainable' phenomenon.

So will these, our transmissions, be declared fantasy by the hard and fast historians, archeologists and astronomers–seekers of hard proof and tangible realities. Yet, you have sought out these teachings because you have tired of their denial, knowing there is so much more to the story of human evolution. Therefore, we salute you for your bravery and your daring to think–to look beyond the confines and see bridges where others do, indeed, see walls.

Children of Atlantis…it is not our purpose to formulate the scientific substance of your belief structures. Many brilliant teachers are drawing the maps, pathways to the lost civilization. Atlantean navigators of the stars, they are today's astro-archeologists, channelers of the Sirian Scientific Commission, trained and prepared to serve this function in your awakening process.

The purpose of these teachings is to stimulate your intuition…the part of you that **remembers**.

You do surely realize that it is no coincidence, your being drawn to the legends of Atlantis, for a fragment of your soul most likely is buried there, attached to the trauma or the glory of a past that lies hidden at the bottom of the seas. If you are 'raising' Atlantis now, it is to gather up the pieces you left behind. This is soul retrieval, a calling back to you the shades of self that have attached to other realities.

You need them all now. You need to integrate Atlantis, together with the fragments left in other lifetimes...other realities. Never before has it been this important to experience yourselves in totality–non-fragmented and whole. It will become clear to you very soon, very soon indeed, as the wheels turn more and more rapidly and you are confronted with the call–the screen images–of those pieces that wish to come 'home'. This, too, is part of the essential process that we refer to as 'clearing and preparing' for the changes ahead of you.

Many incarnated beings walking your planet at this time have come in with unresolved karmic debts, which they intended, as soul essence, to bring to the surface and resolve. This is the pivotal moment when such group process needs to occur on your planet. Our intention is to help guide you through that healing process and call you from your trance for, once again, the dark ones are drawing upon your energies, while you lie sleeping in their opiate fields. You need to hear the untold version of the Atlantean dilemma so that you can extrapolate that which you believe is relevant to your current situation and use it to affect changes in consciousness.

Those changes, understand, will in turn affect the Earth Changes and the ripple continues throughout your solar system, the galaxy, and on to other dimensions. Nothing is separate; all is interdependent in the Cosmos; all souls are united in the perpetual ascension of consciousness.

Perhaps, once you have heard the complete story of the Last Generation–the mind-control mechanisms that were used to harness the energies of the population, and the manipulation of the atmosphere and inner world of Gaia–you will be empowered to lift off the veil and see clearly what lies before you. It is a time of preparation...of shaking off the drug and taking charge.

The human race is a body of six billion units of consciousness, most of whom are predominantly concerned with their individual needs and desires. If a greater concentration of those energies can be used to recognize how you have been separated, and how your ego-centered consciousness has been deliberately manipulated to create within you feelings of isolation and abandonment, you will have taken the initial steps to minimizing the intensity of the Earth Changes.

It is time for you to put together the story of your past so that you can reach an understanding of what has passed before you. In the no-time of the higher dimensions, there is no difference and **only knowledge marks the direction of your time reference.**

We are prepared to offer what insights we can to assist you in your search for the higher truth, but we remind you that it is from within that you will receive absolute affirmation. Yours is the task of reaching that truth and turning it outward for the good of the All.

This is your assignment on Planet Earth.

# Chapter 4

## Nebiru: The Lone Ship

Of the many millennia which mark the rise and fall of the land and beings of Atlantis, we shall be focused primarily upon the period corresponding to Earth's calendar from approximately 27,000 BC to 10,800 BC, to which we shall refer throughout these teachings as the 'third cycle' of Atlantis. This great epoch of Atlantean civilization concludes there, in the final years of the Last Generation, when the dark side held the pendulum and great pockets of humanity across the globe were sacrificed due to the irresponsible abuse of power by the cloaked Priesthood.

Atlantis disappeared deep within the ocean, to rest forever in isolation and oblivion, while other earth lands were engulfed by flood waters, which would retreat in time when the resulting cloud cover lifted and the warmth of Ra, your Sun, could once again be felt on the surface. Of the great continent and its people, however, all that would remain were mythical tales and remote memories; these were handed down, from generation to generation, to those whose ancestry found root in the story of Atlantis.

The monumental cataclysm known to you as the 'Great Flood' was your celestial body's process of cleansing the poisonous energies and altered frequencies emanating from Atlantean control towers and underground energy networks in the final hours. It was Gaia's reaction to the discordant vibrations that radiated from these centers—high into the outer layers of the ionosphere, far across the ley lines of your planet and deep within—disrupting the harmonics of all life at every point of the planet and out into space. They had to be released from Earth's auric field and healed at the core level.

This resulted in the destruction of the perpetrators as well as the 'innocent', for, in ways that are unclear to those of you who have not yet understood karmic process, they contributed to the colossal reaction of the elemental energies that form Gaia's multidimensional body. Remember…all thoughts and actions affect the outcome of all realities. From the omnipotent to the resigned and defeated, all conscious beings actively participate in the creation and playing out of karma.

We, too, have contributed to the karmic debt of Atlantis and, therefore, we have a vested interest in its resolution. You must remember that, as you explore the Atlantean story through our thought frequencies and the words that have been reproduced for you here, via the channel, Trydjya.

As consciousness units, we confront aspects of duality in varying shades and intensities, in order to be free to experience the evolutionary driver of existence: choice. We cannot experience choice without polarity. That, dear ones, is the reason that the dark side even exists. It is there to give us the **freedom** to choose and the **responsibility** for those choices. Therein lies a simple truth, which so empowers us, the conscious units of All-That-Is, that it defies the very existence of 'evil'. Can you own up to it?

You, free will individuals all, can either derive power from the existence of the darkness by **choosing** the Light, the good of the All, or have your power taken by it, by giving yourselves to the shadow…obeying, fearing and exalting the ego (the separate personality self). Once you integrate this aspect of your existence, you will understand the nature of conflict in your lives and how, by viewing all beings as One with you, it can be resolved.

Alien forces were involved in the destruction of Atlantis and they, too, are now faced with the karmic pay-off resulting from their actions. Yet, in many ways, they are still in denial. Here we are referring specifically to the Annunaki warriors of Nebiru, rulers of a technologically advanced, subterranean civilization which exists within a three-dimensional planet body that moves in and out of your solar system every 3,600 years. This eccentric planet, Nebiru, travels in a rather unnatural cyclical path to the outer reaches of Sirius and then back through the dark galactic winter until it re-enters your Sun's orbit. It traverses the body of Ra for a period of approximately thirty earth years and then moves back out again to return to the unknown…the cold journey through deep space.

To understand the deeds and misdeeds of the Annunaki, one must first consider their isolation, for they are, in a sense, the homeless of the galaxy, spending most of their lifetimes far from the light and warmth of Solar Deity, inhabiting the underground cities and military installations of Nebiru's inner being. Their survival depends upon their ability to procure and store necessary life-supporting resources, which they gather during their passing through these respective solar systems, so that they can survive their lone ship's long, dark journey through the universe of matter.

Theirs is a constant search for energy, which they derive primarily from minerals and ores—one essential reason that, throughout time, they have used you to mine the treasures of inner Earth for them. They draw from your emotional, mental and lower astral bodies as well, for there is found an infinite source of energy that feeds the lower chakras, abating their insatiable hunger for more power and control over their own existence. Once you have understood their approach to managing your most precious resources, you will recognize what irony lies in their mindless destruction of the source that fuels them…and how that plays out karmically. You will understand how they have embroiled themselves in the very net they threw around Planet Earth when they first lassoed you.

Like flies in the spider's intricate web, the first *Homo Sapiens* were trapped in the net, stunned by inconsonant electromagnetic frequencies which the Annunaki master engineers wove so tightly around the emotional body of Gaia that it was as if the Goddess could no longer breathe in the light of Prime Creator. It was a dark moment on Earth, in violent opposition to the work of the Elders who had seeded you, and we know now that we helped create it by invading Earth's sovereignty. We do recognize our part and responsibility in the clashing of the dark and light forces at the time of your inception, which set the dynamic precedent for your future...your 'now', which is why we are here for you.

Many of the gifts and capabilities that had been your birthright as the starseeded super race were stripped from you. These were replaced with mechanisms that bind and suppress human thoughts and emotions, holding you locked into 3D, while they scrambled the light frequencies coming in on the Gossamer Web, so that you would somehow forget you were the blessed children of the stars. They were, to a great extent, effective. The new race of Homo Sapiens would still look to the stars for inspiration, but would be denied free access to them and the human race, the Annunaki determined, would remain earth-bound and isolated, for as long as they could sufficiently contain you in their nets.

As we embark upon the study of Annunaki aggression and its effective manipulation of Earth, we ask you to bear in mind that we believe their being isolated in space to be, in many respects, the cause of their persistent ego-centered behavior, which drives them to clutch and take what they want from you. They are out there in the sunless night for most of Nebiru's cyclical passing from one solar system to another, distant observers of worlds in which they can manage to interfere, but never truly **belong**.

At a point in the space-time continuum so distant from your reality as to be undefinable in your terms, a great cosmic exchange occurred in our triunal solar system, which consists of three Solar Deities: Sothis, Satais and Anu (identified by your astronomers, respectively, as Sirius A, Sirius B, and Sirius C.) At the time of this cataclysmic change in our complex stellar body, the deity, Satais, collapsed, passing through her own astral chords and onto higher dimensional planes (much as your own Sun, Ra, is soon to do). What was left behind in the world of matter was, in stellar terms, a minuscule dwarf star of super dense matter, which was eventually pulled into an elliptical orbit around the dominant sister star, Sothis–as was the distant cousin, Anu.

Both continue to create disturbance and gravitational interference in the solar body of the great blue-white star, (the Dog Star) Sothis, which has been seen by your astronomers to wobble and shake from its vibrational exchange with its older siblings.

The collapse of Satais (Sirius B)–its ascension beyond material space–caused a monumental chain reaction through the entire Sirian system, out across the constellation of stars known to you as Canis Major and, indirectly, your solar system became involved in the dynamics of our evolution. For reasons too complex to describe to you at this point in your awareness of celestial dynamics, Nebiru, the most remote planet in Anu's orbit, was knocked off its rotational path in the process and sent careening through space to eventually be grabbed by the gravitational pull of your star, Ra, drawn into your solar system, and then ricocheted back out into space. Other planet bodies circling Anu held their orbits, surviving the shock wave, while the planets orbiting Satais (Sirius B) were sucked into the vortex and through her astral chord, ascending with the Deity onto higher dimensional planes.

Such a colossal 'boomerang' theory and the ensuing idea of sunless planets surviving in space may sound utterly preposterous to you, given your current understanding of astrophysics, but we ask you to bear in mind that you still observe the Universe from a 3D vantage point, where everything must somehow fit with your rather fixed ideas of how things 'work' in your own 'earthly' reality. The movements of the celestial bodies are enormously different than they are believed to be from the viewing stations of Planet Earth. Consider that your perspective is rather myopic, for you still experience your world as the center of the Universe–just as your forefathers believed it a flatland from which you could reach the edge and fall away into nothingness.

With the discovery of quantum physics, your scientific community is re-defining humanity's command of celestial mechanics and the inner space of the subatomic realms...and what may contradict all the known 'laws' of science today very probably will be the discoveries of tomorrow.

The Power's top scientists have already bridged that gap. So stretch your minds a bit–and be daring. Glide around in the 'possibility' zone where your acquired knowledge, education and convictions do not automatically reject new perspectives–such as those we are declaring here to be the workings of the Cosmos, as they are known to us.

The celestial dynamics of Sirius, combined with the alignments of key celestial bodies of your galaxy and the entry of Nebiru into your solar system, were in great part responsible for cataclysmic events which took place upon Earth and at other points in your solar system then, and they are still the catalysts of change within your greater solar family now. With the perennial passing of the turnabout, Nebiru, between us, we have established resonance with your Solar Deity and become, in ways that are significant to our mutual evolution, linked with the forces of Ra.

We remind you that, of all the planetary bodies of Ra, Earth was the most fascinating...particularly to Sirians, whose planetary homes exhibit geo-physical properties very similar to yours. The blue-green planet was the ultimate Eden, rich in minerals and bio-diversity, and the Nebiruans were drawn to you for the time they passed through your solar system. They soon realized that Earth had all the potential to provide them with a wealth of resources that they could no longer harvest from their home planet's uninhabitable surface. Indeed, they set their designs on Earth, believing they had found a New World for future generations of Nebiruans–just as you have begun to look to Mars for yours.

Many other extraterrestrial civilizations were attracted to Gaia, for she sang out to be heard. The communication chakra of your Solar Deity, she called upon the intelligence of the Universe to be seeded with the hope of birthing a superior race of conscious light beings. Bear in mind that our Elders were key players in the Great Experiment, which resulted in the appearance of *Homo Sapiens* upon the Earth...but know that our connection to you began far earlier in time, when our Deity, Satais, passed through her astral chord to experience ascension. Nebiru, flung out of its orbit and pulled into the magnetic field of Ra, eventually became the galactic messenger between our two Solar Deities. These were the true beginnings of the open exchange between us.

Therefore, we must remember in our discussion of the Nebiruans that, although they interfered with the Great Work of the Elders, they have strengthened our connection to you on material planes and we are grateful to them for having served this purpose. Exiled from our star system, they have deposited Sirian codes within many civilizations and ancient worlds, most clearly recorded in the temples of Egypt.

We observe you as you move in great numbers now to explore the land of the Pharaohs, experiencing your shifting emotional bodies and connecting with you at those sites. This is as we intended, for the great works of that ancient civilization hold the records of your true history, just as they hold the story of your future. There are found six-dimensional Sirian codes, five-dimensional Pleiadian ascension constructs and Nebiruan records and frequencies. Although there exist many other points of convergence upon (and within) your planet, Egypt remains the most elaborate multidimensional library currently accessible in the three-dimensional fields of Earth's memory.

Your guides and seers are beginning to decipher the messages that will assist you at this time of searching for the Knowledge. Sirian records are of the no-time, for we exist beyond the limitations of linear time, and so the 'future' is written, as is the 'past'. Your comprehension of the no-time will be essential to the breaking of the codes. There has been progress; you have recognized in many of the hieroglyphic representations of the Egyptian gods and goddesses the celestial workings of the Universe. The story, the Cosmos of universal soul, is concealed in the vestments of the neteru; for centuries you have been deciphering how the deities depicted in the tombs and temples are actually representations of celestial beings and events as they were understood at that time.

The Nebiruans played a key role in bringing to the civilization the technological knowledge to build the great monuments and extraterrestrial constructs—records of their passing amongst you—while we came into that reality on other levels. There, too, they created control structures, generated lower vibrational electromagnetic frequencies and imposed belief systems, whereas Sirian and Pleiadian energies were working to expand and accelerate Egyptian awareness. Never before, not even in Atlantis, has there been such multidimensional imprinting upon the collective human psyche.

As you feel and internalize the vibrational codes in the Egyptian temples traveling a wide expanse of emotions and shifting awareness, remember that all is not light in the Pharaonic fields. Ancient Nebiruan control devices are still operating there and you must pay attention that you are not flooded at their gates. These are the masters of control frequencies and they have left their signature in those lands knowing, as did we, that you would find your way to the record halls. These are the strongest in the Nile Temple of Kom Ombo and Elephantine Island, yet you have much to gain from entering those fields and raising the vibration to receive the knowledge encoded there. There are many overlays, many layers to be traversed and processed from your passage, and you will want to be tuning in at the higher levels.

The Annunaki still operate in these realms through electromagnetic pulse technologies, etheric imprinting and holographic imaging. Therefore, be sure to carry the unconditional love of Spirit into the sites and remember that your vibrations remain in the ethers. Moreover, consider how the frequencies that you experience leave their imprint upon your auric fields. Dedicating yourselves to the light, while creating the appropriate protective shields around you, is going to be ever more necessary to you now, when you approach any site of worship, energy vortex or altered state of consciousness.

What becomes significant in our discussion of the Annunaki is how their planet's continual re-entry into your system coincides with periods of great upheaval and monumental change upon the Earth. Visitations from the Annunaki have marked the following key time frames in your solar system's history:

450,000 years ago, the Nebiruans first visit Earth, returning at regular intervals since then, approximately every 3,600 years.

97,200 BC (The Annunaki intervene in the Great Experiment–the seeding of *Homo Sapiens*.)

32,400 BC (Nebiru's entry into your solar system coincides with other celestial events which cause Planet Earth to flip its axis, initiating your most recent Ice Age.)

28,800 BC (the second cycle of Atlantis comes to a close with the glaciation of the continent.)

25,200 BC (the Annunaki establish military bases on Mars.)

21,600 BC (Annunaki transit stations are created on the Moon.)

18,000 BC (the first Annunaki settlements in the land known to you as Africa establish mining colonies of precious ores.)

14,400 BC (the Annunaki land in Atlantis, which coincides with the beginnings of opposition in the Priesthood.)

10,800 BC (Atlantis disappears below the ocean.)

7,200 BC (the Annunaki appear in Mesopotamia, intervening in the Sumerian civilization.)

3,600 BC (the Annunaki intervene in Egypt, a civilization established through direct intervention with Sirian and Pleiadian Light Emissaries.)

ZERO TIME (the birthing of the Christed One.)

Calculating a 3,600 year cycle, it is clear that the lone planet is not scheduled back into your solar system in time for the Mayan date of December 21, 2012 AD. This is of particular significance to the cosmic unfolding of events occurring at that projected point in the space-time continuum and devastating to the Nebiruans. Just as before, with the collapse of Satais, all heavenly bodies orbiting the ascending star will be pulled through the black hole and into the higher dimension. Nebiru, however, will be out there in galactic winter, at a remote point somewhere between the Sirius star system and yours, neither close enough to be pulled through with you, nor near enough to Sirius to grab orbit in our system. They are fearful, worried about their fate, and they are searching desperately for a solution.

The Annunaki are well aware of what their technologies have generated upon the Earth, for they have not forgotten the sinking of Atlantis and the silencing of vast expanses of life that resulted at many points of the globe. Nor have they forgotten their devastation of the Martian atmosphere, after their rape of that planet resulted in the destruction of its auric field…just as it is destroying your ozone and upper atmosphere.

They were the builders of the ancient city brought to your attention by the adept, Richard Hoagland, who revealed NASA's photo images of what are the remains of their central temple complex on Mars. For many of you, these striking images are the undeniable proof that there is intelligent life beyond your boundaries. Despite the Space Agency's insistence that the 'face' which most clearly looks out at you from the Martian terrain is but an optical illusion, the Nebiruan Sphinx is there, just as real and commanding as the great lioness of Giza, and just as mysterious.

Unfortunately, their plundering of the resources of Mars and their disregard for its environment resulted in the almost total destruction of the life-sustaining energy fields of the planet's surface. And yet, they have learned nothing. Under Annunaki rule, enforced upon you by their progeny, Earth is about to lose its atmosphere as well, and this you are already experiencing as holes in the ozone and drastic alteration of the ionosphere. At the polar ice caps you are seeing the breaking up of the glacial masses, which have begun to migrate out into your oceans and this, you understand, can only lead to further flooding and ecological consequence.

They tell you there is no proof of global warming. We are telling you that depletion of the ozone–Earth's 'life support system'–is occurring much more rapidly than you realize and that you are making no progress towards remedying the crisis. Worse, the latest technologies involving the deliberate heating of the ionosphere, together with the proliferation of nuclear-powered satellites around the planet, are speeding up the process of atmospheric disintegration.

Do you wonder why the leaders of your world refuse to address environmental issues with any seriousness, considering the imminent disaster awaiting Planet Earth? Look to this explanation for an answer to your frustrated cries for ecological resolutions from the governments that rule you: it is not in the interest of the Annunaki lords. They are intent upon taking all there is from you, to prepare for their own salvation in the wake of what is about to take place in your Sun's body, rippling all the way through the galaxy.

Curtailing their rapacious theft of your vital resources for the sake of the environment and the living of Gaia is simply not part of their private agenda. It never has been. Unfortunately, their ego-centered consciousness, their feelings of isolation and the cold darkness of their endless wheel in space do not allow them to care about your problems in any other ways but those which directly affect their own interests.

Over 450,000 years ago, Nebiru entered extremely close to Earth in its course through your solar system. From their galactic viewing station, the Annunaki observed the blue-green planet and, not unlike Columbus, your heroic explorer, decided that they, too, had 'discovered' a New World. It was determined that Earth would be claimed as their own. Once Nebiru moved close enough into range that they could affect a full-scale probe of the planet, the Annunaki boarded their 'great sailing ships' and moved in for a closer look, surprised to find a remote, undeveloped planet–bursting with unlimited plant and animal species–with no visible signs of an intelligent civilization.

This, to beings of the much older star system of Sirius, was a revolutionary discovery. It was foreign to their perception of a universe known to be teeming with intelligent life that a host planet of such rich resources had not yet been cultivated by a sentient species–one at least superior to the animals they encountered during their first landing missions.

They left Planet Earth to its natural evolutionary process, hoping to see great leaps in your progress with each return into your solar system, for they knew that one day they would need intelligent life forms to produce energy for them. To the Annunaki, Earth was now their private real estate, and they set their intention to develop the property, checking in on its progress from time to time, as was facilitated by their new course through the 3D universe.

With each cyclical re-entry into the body of Ra, the Nebiruans discovered more about the planets that joined Earth in their orbit around your Sun. As with Mars, they did investigate and colonize other celestial bodies in the solar system, but you were always the target and focus of their interest, for Earth was the most appetizing. They observed the changing face of Gaia, studying the flora and fauna of her vast virgin lands. Like curious scientists, they occasionally intervened in Earth's process with technologies that belonged to your future, mutating the natural progression of the life forms that abounded at that stage to fit their future needs of the planet.

At a much later point in their many returns to the far reaches of our stellar body, they got wind of the Great Experiment being planned for Gaia, and became outraged. They believed that we were interfering in their territorial domain, for they had watched and waited for Earth to reach the point where they could harvest her resources and they had their own ideas for genetic intervention on your planet. These involved potentially mixing their own seed with that of the primate, Homo Erectus, to create an intelligent brute force to mine and work the Earth for them.

Their first experiments had been promising. When news of the successful seeding of *Homo Sapiens*, the super race of light beings, reached their sentinels, it was decided that the only way they would retain control over their new domain was by sabotaging the new human race, so that they might drive our attention away from Planet Earth forever.

It may shock you to hear that the first extraterrestrial abductions occurred one hundred thousand years ago, when the Annunaki teams descended upon the Earth and rewired your DNA, disabling ten of the twelve strands that were part of your original make-up: your light coding. You were raped of your immense potential, stripped to the bare bones required for your survival as a race and as future subjects of Annunaki rule. Their intentions for your planet simply did not allow for a sudden, super race of multidimensional beings upsetting their plans for an eventual take-over of the planet.

Obviously, they knew that those who had birthed you were, in a sense, attending to your incubation in the warm nest of Gaia's light. In those halcyon days of your emergence, Homo Sapiens, the Light Ones of the Universe were focused upon you, celebrating your future as the new curators of the solar system in which you reside, for it was your destiny to reach greatness within and beyond the limits of your realm.

They, the Annunaki, knew we would respond to their invasive act—the sabotaging of the Great Experiment—but they were in a position to act quickly. Once the bio-geneticists had completed their mission, their engineers threw a grid around the planet, an immense force field that created such dissonant waves that, in fact, we found we were unable to reach resonance with you. Although, with time, we have been able to adjust our frequency to penetrate the weakening field and get through to growing numbers of you, the grid still surrounds your world and it continues to plague you. It has caused great disruption of Earth, while disturbing you on many levels...particularly there, where it interacts with Gaia's own electromagnetic vortex points.

Fortunately, as you will understand in later lessons, the acceleration of your ascending Solar Deity is causing such disturbance in the grid that it is finally about to break apart, releasing all earth beings from its grip. This is a necessary and natural part of your evolution at this time of your transmutation out of the third dimension.

Why, one asks, did the Annunaki commit such a violent act against the virgin lands and beings of Earth? Quite simply, they were resentful of you...and this has not changed, despite all that they have perpetrated upon you. To the Annunaki of Nebiru, you were the 'favorite child' of the Universe—the special breed—those who were handed everything while they, the outcasts, had to clutch and take what they could to survive. You have known the Garden of Eden and the radiance of the Sun, and even though they are, in many ways, responsible for your destructive approach to the management of Earth's resources, they cannot forgive you for your indifference in the face of such abundance. That is the paradox. And so, they believe they can take what they want from you. And so, indeed, they have...yet most of your world has never even noticed.

While the Annunaki lords of Nebiru confront their fate, their descendants, the power elite, are feverishly planning their own salvation. They are currently directing the preparation of the Moon for full-scale invasion for, according to their informers (the gray technicians), Earth will soon be wiped clean of all life forms as she passes through the tunnel of Ra's rebirthing. They believe that the Moon, still relatively undisturbed and clear of Earth's chaotic frequencies, will be a safer bet for their passage.

Knowing what they and their progeny are creating within the mental, emotional and physical bodies of the human race, and well aware of what they have done to Gaia, they have it as a foregone conclusion that nothing upon your planet will survive the shift. To those of the dark intention, it could appear to be so, for they are focused on that which isn't right about you and your world. Accustomed to the darkness, they are drawn to their own murky reflection; what they are seeing is actually a mirror of what they created for themselves before...when Sirius B ascended and they were sent spinning out into the darkness of galactic night.

We wish to clarify that, when referring to the Annunaki, we are speaking of the dark forces of Nebiru–the warriors of Anu–but we ask you to bear in mind that there, too, dark and light forces are at work. There are many different vibrational patterns of soul consciousness on that planet. We are not attempting to mount a campaign against the Nebiruans, for we understand the foundations of their envy and their rage and we empathize with them.

**We feel compassion for those who choose to linger in the dark shadows.**

Their free will choices as a race have bound them to a karmic pattern that is incredibly slow in evolving spiritually. But as we have told you, all conscious beings carry the spark of Prime Creator. There, too, are mothers and nurturing ones, who fear and tremble in the dark hours of their journey, and they are beings of the All-That-Is: no less than you; no less than we.

If you wish to emerge from your suffering and repression, you must never forget that we are all expressions of the Divine: sparks of the Creator. You must never close down your heart centers, forgetting to forgive the other, for each has an agenda of growth and awakening; each has an expression and a rhythm. This is not the way of the light and we remind you that now, more than ever, the brilliance of your love and compassion for all beings is needed if you are to raise the frequencies of your world.

All of your nemeses—the phantoms and dark ones—are somewhere along the path that leads back to the Godhead. It is of utmost importance that you recognize this spiritual truth, now that you are uncovering the intentions of the ruling elite and what they have done to you in the past. It is important to your understanding of what went wrong in Atlantis and it is essential now that you are preparing to reclaim the power and set yourselves free.

There is no place for fear here. There is no place for rage. These dark emotions only bring you into resonance with the lowest Annunaki vibrations. Can you see how you draw them into you?

By recognizing their emotional patterns, you can understand how they move about in your mental and emotional bodies and how they take from you. You can see how they have successfully held the Earth for so many thousands of years. The controls are weakening now, as the original grid rapidly disintegrates, and in their panic they are looking to the Moon for immediate solutions and beyond—to Mars—for 'permanence'. Quite naturally, the time has never been better to release yourselves from their hold. With their attention diverted from Earth, you, the lightworkers of Gaia, are freer to concentrate upon raising the frequency to a level where they can no longer reach you and, in so doing, the light of all of Gaia will become brighter.

You will have to 'un-plug' some of the control devices and turn down the others if you wish to succeed in this full-scale effort. You must release yourselves from their nets while pulling the masses up out of the deep waters.

It will not be enough to hold the wisdom and the way for your own edification, detaching yourselves...like hermits in the caves. The era of your isolation has all but ended. All the heart of humanity is needed now. This is the time for union.

In fairness, we must acknowledge that the intentions of the Nebiruans have not only been dark and controlling. They have participated in many ways to the evolution of your race, bringing the ancients untold knowledge of the galaxy, technological preparation light years ahead of humankind's development and an all-too-keen awareness of the mineral resources available to them. To your modern world, they have contributed many technologies that have, in a sense, served for the betterment of life on your planet. And, as we mentioned earlier, they have brought us closer, serving as cosmic messengers between Sirius and Ra for many hundreds of thousands of earth years.

Nonetheless, the Annunaki's 'contributions' have been conditional. They have been doled out to the human race as part of their recipe for global dominion. You can understand how the ancients were fooled. Would they have expected such behavior from 'gods'? In those innocent days of idyllic Atlantis, could the idle priests have imagined just how much they were giving away? Could they have known how the dark force would devastate the human spirit, sending the entire continent–your world–into a cataclysm of such magnitude? And of the future of Atlantis...could they have foreseen the karmic unfolding of their acts of subordination to the Annunaki lords: the social unrest, mental and emotional conflict, disease and disruption of the world of the future? Considering their highly-developed awareness, couldn't they have prevented being taken in and exploited?

At the time of the Annunaki's direct intervention in the third cycle of Atlantis (at around 14,400 BC.), some of the Priesthood, grown complacent from the elitist lifestyle afforded them as spirit leaders of the land, began to feel the need for mental and emotional stimulation.

They had inherited much knowledge from the early civilizations and the innate wisdom of the ancient priestesses. Many were direct line descendants of those who we will simply refer to for the moment as the 'Keepers of the Crystals'. All initiates trained in the teachings of the Elders, keeping alive their multidimensional understanding of the properties of crystals and minerals, which was to form the basis of their modern technology, reaching and surpassing areas very similar to those you are developing now.

By the middle of the third cycle, they had developed their knowledge to such an extent that they had learned to illuminate the entire continent with crystal-powered generators. They had created sea and air-going vessels, tapped solar energies and delved profoundly into the harnessing of the collective mind as a catalyst for much of their technology. They heated their homes with solar energy and processed their nominal waste in biological recycling centers, so that nothing disturbed the environment of their idyllic lands. They, the High Priests of Atlán, utilized their knowledge for the good of the people, while maintaining that ancestral respect for the habitat in which they lived and prospered. So what went wrong?

Understand that in that phase of your social advancement where humankind challenges its capabilities and takes the enormous anthropological leaps focused upon 'conquering' the elements, the predominant energies at work are of the yang vibration...a time of thrusting forward. That is invigorating, especially to the male species because it gets, shall we say, the testosterone flowing. Once the drivers of a given civilization reach the apex, where there is nothing left to conquer but each other, one witnesses the decline of the civilization, which will tear down its creations, destroying itself so that it can be reborn and rebuilt again. This is the way of life not only upon the Earth, but on many stations in material space as well. As it sinks into the final hours of its self-imposed annihilation, the dying civilization once again reverts to the nurturing, healing energies of the yin vibration and the cycle eventually begins anew.

The civilization of Nebiru is the exception to the paradigm for, in its desperate struggle for survival, it has yet to reach the apex point. The Nebiruans are so obsessed with their need as a race to make it back into either solar system that, for them, the pendulum has yet to swing. The thrusting, aggressive force is the very nature of the planet, for it has no Sun to mirror...only glimpses of the light, and so it has become the overriding energy of the entire race. This may help you to understand why they have imposed survival behavior upon you as well.

Nebiru's re-entry into your solar system at 14,400 BC coincided with just such an apex point in Atlantean evolution, when the dominant yang vibration was beginning to wane. Those of the Priesthood, whose leadership had gradually acquired a material focus, were becoming bored with their creations. They still believed they were working for the good of the people, but their perspective of what was 'good' for society had become clouded by their technological prowess and a progressive shifting away from spiritual values.

The Annunaki seized the opportunity, landing their shuttle ships in Atlantean territories and presenting themselves to the High Priests as gods from the heavens: a seemingly 'divine' intervention. Experts in aggressive mind-altering technologies, they immediately found an open highway for the establishing of resonant thought patterning, with which they were able to enter into the individual energy fields of some of the less evolved of the Atlantean Priesthood.

Hyperactivation of their power chakras was performed by the Annunaki lords, who plugged in to the ego consciousness of the priests, stimulating and fueling their restlessness, until soon a dissonant frequency began to create disharmony within the Priesthood. While the Light Ones regarded the arrival of the Annunaki with circumspection, others were being secretly trained in new technologies that were initially presented as 'gifts' for humankind. However, what was really being offered the mutating priests were the tokens of a **New World Order.**

They, the priests of the New Order, paved the way to the establishing of the Dark Priesthood—polar forces to the High Priests of Ra. Goaded by the Annunaki, they became determined not only to hold power over their former brothers and all the peoples of their growing dominion, but they grew to believe that they should expand their influence to reach further across the seas.

In a short time, they were pushing past their boundaries, always seeking to increase their influence and to mine the resources of other civilizations. The more they gave the Annunaki gods in worship, the more knowledge that was bestowed upon them…knowledge intended to help them achieve total world domination under Annunaki rule.

**We wonder if that might just ring familiar to you.**

Genetic engineering techniques were secretly introduced to the new dark of the Priesthood at that time. Their first covert experiments involved implanting Annunaki seed into select human females to bring forth the first generations of Earth-born Nebiruans, and they were successful. These, the first test tube babies of Atlantis, were fertilized 'in vitro' and implanted into the women. You may have already intuited that the contemporary practice of artificial insemination is simply Annunaki technology deliberately re-introduced into human consciousness and implemented at this time for reasons that should be clear as well.

These, the first genetically structured, Nebiruan-fathered male infants, were taken from their mothers immediately and raised in total isolation by Annunaki guardians, just as those deemed to be warriors are taken on their home planet. They were brought up in a strict military environment and trained in the most sophisticated methodologies, for they were to become the new administrators of the Dark Priesthood and the ultimate rulers of Atlantis. Their seed would, in turn, bring in the next generation of Annunaki lords, overseers of the Earth station, and still others would follow, guiding the course of the entire human race to serve the needs of Nebiru.

Such ambition left no room for the kind of complacency and emotional well-being that typified most of the Atlantean populace at that time. Their rearing of the new breed was based on one fundamental precept: that to become omnipotent rulers, they would have to be taught from birth to want more, so that they could be driven to take more.

They were taught mind-control technologies that were to be implemented in the culture, a civilization that had trained for millennia in the focusing of thought within the crystal generators that appeared across the great expanse of the continent. It was, in essence, a civilization ripe for the taking and the Annunaki were hungry after their long passage through the galactic night. They would draw upon the energies of the collective to fuel their intention and manipulate the dark priests through their power centers. They would own the human race.

It was these predominant ego-driven energies of the Dark Priesthood, and (as we shall describe in later transmissions) the team of alchemists who were fueled by the Annunaki, which were directly responsible for unleashing Gaia's fury. Despite the enormous efforts of the Atlantean lightworkers to raise the vibration, the consciousness of the masses sank into resignation, servitude and despair. The light of the Priesthood began to fade, marking a turning point in the destiny of the Atlanteans and that of future societies of Planet Earth.

The wanton abuse of the dark priests and their careless manipulation of frequency and vibration altered the four elements of your planet to such a point that the seas expanded, land masses collapsed and the skies blackened in the shadow of volcanic dust. Like the cold death of nuclear winter, all fell silent upon the face of the Earth, a planet shrouded in clouds and darkness. Incessant were the rains, relentless and violent, for the natural balance of Gaia had been destroyed by the misguided magic of the dark warriors, and only total purification and renewal would restore the flow–the life essence–to her being.

# Chapter 5

## The Yzhnüni

### The Second Cycle

How possibly could the dark minority of the Atlantean Priesthood have so drastically altered the evolution of an entire planet? Before we can effectively describe the events leading to the cataclysm of the Last Generation, we must briefly take you back to a time of a much earlier Atlantean society, when living conditions and the cultural development of the continent, by your current standards, would have been considered 'primitive'.

We speak of a time in the second cycle of Atlantean civilization, ending with the glacial freeze of the ensuing Ice Age, which had engulfed vast areas of the Earth in dense ice sheets up to three miles in depth. It had consumed Atlantean shores and midlands by around 28,600 BC, silencing all life in those regions for over one thousand years, when rapid deglaciation sent the melting ice running into the oceans surrounding the continent and, despite the flooding of the coastal areas and the low lands, life in the higher grounds sprung anew.

Thrown off-balance by the extreme magnetic shifting in the celestial bodies which held resonance with Earth at the time of Nebiru's re-entry (around 32,000 BC), your planet literally flipped its axis, re-defining the north and south poles and dramatically altering the climate, land masses and waters of Gaia. Some areas were devoured by huge glacial sheets in what you could consider 'an instant', bringing almost all life upon the surface to a frozen halt for many thousands of years. At other points of the planet, the encroaching ice sheets engulfed much of the land much more slowly…thousands of years after the cataclysmic shifting of the poles.

At those locations where *Homo Sapiens* had time to react to the climatic aberration, there was a great migration to the high grounds of the yet uncovered land masses: places such as the Himalayas and the Andes. There were survivors.

One such location was the continent of Atlantis.

\*                    \*                    \*

Prior to the freezing of Atlantis, the natives lived as an extension of the natural environment, in relative harmony with the Earth. They had reached a highly evolved state of being in light body, capable of time travel and astral journeying at will. Their ancestors had grown up side-by-side with the wild beasts and creatures that populated the planet at that stage of Gaia's development, and early in their evolution they learned to domesticate certain animals that served to protect and assist in their survival.

Never did the second cycle Atlanteans eat animal flesh. Some domesticated animals were utilized for their milk and others for their eggs: these were considered gifts from the 'four legged creatures'. The mainstay of their diet, however, was found in the verdant habitant of the continent, rich in many forms of fruits and nuts, herbs and medicinal beings, for they sensed that the light captured within the leaves provided the electrical charge of Solar Deity, while the roots offered the magnetic grounding energies of the Earth Mother…and it was so.

From a spiritual context, that constituted a highly developed state of awareness—a higher vibration—when humankind had a much clearer understanding of the nature of all living beings. Moreover, they had respect for the All: the rocks; the ocean beings; the great trees and animals; each other. All were considered reflections of Prime Creator and nothing was taken from the environment without permission. Not even a fruit was plucked without the blessing of the tree, for the early Atlanteans enjoyed telepathic interaction with all the life forms that shared their environment. There was an ultimate respect between all living things and Nature was gracious…as was man.

Native Americans (those who have not been beaten into submission by the self-appointed lords of their lands–the Annunaki headquarters) still retain many of their ancestral ways. The Hopi have been the most successful Keepers of the Records of the second cycle Atlanteans, but all the natives of the Americas hold that wisdom in their ancestral ways and tribal memory. Your access to the native speakers of all indigenous peoples is the closest you can come to understanding that state of oneness that humankind once shared with all the living of Gaia.

Free of disease and pacifist in nature, the second cycle Atlanteans lived much longer life spans than you have imagined possible on your planet. Allusion has been made in your Holy Scriptures, there where the rulers of modern religion have not destroyed the evidence in the re-writing of the ancient texts. It was not uncommon to live up to one thousand of your Earth years. In fact, in many environments in material space, life spans of physical beings tend to be substantially longer than those you currently experience on Earth.

Those of Nebiru, for example, span almost two millennia and that is a reflection of the conditions with which they must contend. Average life expectancies of living forms alter constantly, affected by many variables in the environment, technology, cosmic events and, more specifically, the collective consciousness.

Consider that only a very few years ago, the average life expectancy of a human being was no more than forty years, yet your contemporary aged are reaching well into their eighties. That is a doubling of the age expectancy in a period of little more than two or three hundred years. If you can fathom tens of thousands of years of evolution, it may be easier for you to accept that things were very, very different on Planet Earth at a time so remote to you that nothing remains in the record.

What you currently believe to be the 'antiquities' of humanity are but grains of sand in the hourglass.

*     *     *

The second cycle Atlanteans had highly-developed psychic and intuitive capabilities and their spiritual focus was Earth-centered, although they worshipped the stars and celestial bodies of the heavens, by which they charted time and their place in a galaxy of star beings. Starseed, they held the knowledge of their stellar origins in the DNA, as do you.

There was no religious hierarchy, for theirs was a direct line to Prime Creator, whom they worshipped in trees, the rivers and seas, birds, the sky and mountaintops. Every day bought new challenges from nature, and these they accepted as Spirit moving through them.

Throughout the existence of human beings upon the Earth, none have ever known such love for Gaia as those of the second cycle of Atlantis. They were totally in tune with other life forms, the elemental energies and the forces of the Cosmos. One can, therefore, imagine their perplexity and terror when the forces of nature seemed, for all intensive purposes, to turn against them.

## The Third Cycle

We reiterate that the third and final cycle began with the melting of the ice sheets. As the glaciers began their rapid retreat from the continent, a great flourishing occurred rather spontaneously and Atlantis, one of the last land masses to experience the devastation, was one of the first to be revitalized…both energetically and climatically. Many Sirian souls chose to generate upon the Earth at that time to assist in the rebirthing of the human race as part of our karmic bond with you, and to settle our unresolved karmic issues with the Annunaki of Nebiru. We were able to read the Akashic Record and observed that the Family of Light would be called into Earth's fields at that time, and so it was believed, in a sense, to be our destiny to incarnate below our vibration in a return to the third dimension.

This was a time when the first Sirians appeared as humanoids upon the face of the Earth, specifically in the mountain lands of Atlantis. Like our Solar Deity, Satais (Sirius B), the planet body of their origin, Yzhnü, is no longer of the material universe, for it resonates at a higher frequency—a six-dimensional planetary essence which exists in a parallel universe alongside of yours. For the Yzhnüni, it was a chance to live again in form, with all the challenges consciously evolving beings would face from the elements, the other life forms and the transmutational process of retrogradation, while resolving the karma that, binding Sirius to the Gaian vibration, would have forever delayed our own evolution.

The Yzhnüni, starseed of Sirius, experienced great difficulty crystallizing in the third dimension, for theirs was a vibration which had long before passed from physicality and the return to material form was riddled with uncertainly. Yet, reports of the blue-green planet, her majesty and music, sang through the universe and her fascination was immense. Quite simply, Gaia was the siren of the heavens and these Sirian souls were the Ulysses of the galactic seas.

Their essence crystallized in the three-dimensional fields of Earth reality as very tall, radiant hominids, of a form that closely resembled human anatomy and structure…but which clearly was not. Most distinguishing were their extensive auric fields, which emanated visibly many feet beyond their physical bodies. Their outer coverings were like a delicate foil, absolutely white and translucent, so that to the natives they appeared as fairy-like beings and were perceived as such for many centuries of their existence in the Earth sphere. They had enormous, bright eyes, which reflected the color indigo; their hair was of the golden white light; their eight-foot tall bodies were slender, delicate and lithe.

The Yzhnüni resonated most closely to the Earth element of water, for their planet was abundant in it, as are the other natural satellites in the Sirian system. In order to hold the Gaian frequency, they were germinated in the highlands of the continent of Atlantis, for there were innumerable caves and grottoes in which they could find the warmth and moisture that best replicated their natural environment, while protecting them from the radiation emitted by the powerful rays of your Solar Deity. It was a terrain that most closely typified the crystalline fields of Yzhnü.

With their first appearance upon the Earth, the Yzhnüni were of such a high vibratory frequency that they could not hold form in the density of your planetary field, nor could they bear any contact with the direct rays emanating from the Sun. To observers, they would have appeared to fade in and out of reality, and they did, indeed, bleed out of the world of matter and back into the sixth dimension repeatedly, until they were finally capable of holding 3D frequency. Their outer sheaths contained none of the pigment required to protect them from the damaging ultraviolet light, and so they were underground in the sunlight hours during those early days of their 'distant' migration.

In time, as this Sirian seed took root in three-dimensional reality, their physical beings became denser and more adapted to Earth's geothermal forces and its relationship to the Sun, which once again shone brilliantly through Earth's atmosphere. Their bodies became more solid and resilient, their skin became more opaque and their coloring took on slightly deeper hues…a somewhat less translucent quality.

Yzhnüni God consciousness was simple and pure, for (as evolved souls in a state of retrogradation) they understood their own divinity just as they recognized the Creator in the elements, and so all worship celebrated their connection with the primordial energies. Power points, the Gaian altars, were centered around those locations where the four elements of your planet interacted: there where volcanic magna erupted from below the freezing seas and then, falling back unto itself, raised new lands in the ever-changing landscape. To witness the fire of the molten earth, steam, the ocean's cooling embrace and the hardening of magma into rock was the most sacred of rituals, for there was the totality of the Goddess of earthly life as it was understood at that time of their Gaian experience.

Further, the process of crystallization—vapor to liquid, magma to stone—evoked within them the memory of their ancestral home (a land of crystalline terrain and vaporous waters). It reminded them of their higher purpose: the soul's commitment to return to the material realm, bringing form to their spiritual ideal of assisting in the evolution of Planet Earth.

There, in the primeval temples of Atlantis, the star children of Sirius first integrated the ancestral note of Sirian soul music, the wam, with the pulsating heartbeat of Gaia, and fusion was made...to be handed down over time and remembered. That sound, the primordial vibration of harmonious wam frequencies, has held open the portals since the birthing of civilization on your planet. Yet, of the power of sonic frequencies you, of the westernized world, still have little or no knowledge.

We ask that you consider with due circumspection how the Keepers of the Frequencies—The Tibetans, the Australian Aborigines, the Native Americans—have all been systematically driven from their sacred lands. There, in their native environments, they drew strength from the earth, resonating to the frequencies of their native fields. Their ancestral memory of sound has helped hold the planet in balance, and we wonder if you recognize in their slow extermination the waves of disharmony that have contributed to the devastation that now surrounds you.

Later generations of Yzhnüni, those who migrated from the colder climates down to the more temperate zones of the continent, still required protection from the ultraviolet rays of the Sun. For this reason, they were drawn to seek shelter and protection in the caves and passageways which typified the rugged terrain, with its multitudinous underground lakes and streams. There, they soon discovered towering quartz caves and fertile valleys of the midlands, which for them proved the most suitable environment available on Earth. By the middle of the third cycle of the Atlantean civilization, they had all settled in these areas of the continent, living within the crystal caves and their surrounding networks of underground passageways…an endless labyrinth of tunnels, grottoes and caverns.

Of this relatively brief appearance of Sirian beings in Atlantean culture, many myths circulated amongst the indigenous tribes…stories of the 'fairy people' who glowed in the night, illuminating the forests and mountain peaks of Atlantis. Yet, any attempt by the natives to approach the Yzhnüni would send them vanishing into thin air…bleeding out of material space and onto astral planes. One can imagine the wonder their presence evoked in a tribal environment of survivalists, a fascination that you have seen revitalized by the Druids of your last millennia and the reappearance of Wicca worshippers in your modern age.

Their nocturnal emergence from the caves was of such luminosity that they could be perceived from far distances–from the valleys below to the high grounds–and quite naturally the people understood them to be of supernatural origins. Still, they were worshipped, rather than feared, and so left undisturbed by the locals, whose primary concerns were of survival in the wild lands of those rugged years of Earth time, much more than of things mystical and unexplainable in their co-existing framework of harsh environmental realities.

With time, these Sirian beings slowly emerged from their crystalline sanctuaries, assuming a much more influential role in the spiritual development of the people by bringing to them their six-dimensional awareness of the Cosmos, the All-That-Is and the evolutionary journey of all consciousness along the Spiral of Light. They were superb teachers, visionaries for a world returning from the frozen tombs of glacial winter, and it was their mission to assist the new generations in rediscovering the spiritual significance of the life that once again abounded around them.

We believe that their greatest gift to the early Atlanteans of the third cycle was their higher knowledge of the energetic properties of the mineral world. While the indigenous people know a great reverence for the life force within all of Earth's beings, select natives (the first priestesses) were eventually shown how to develop a much more profound understanding of the rocks and crystals of Gaia as elemental beings, amplifiers of energy, generators and storehouses of light. This knowledge was to serve the spiritual and technological advancement of the people, while opening the portals of multidimensionality. The Yzhnüni introduced to that culture their understanding of frequency, the nature of matter and the elements, the powers of telepathic communication and the process of teleportation–catapulting the Atlantean civilization far ahead of the rest of the world in an evolutionary theater of intergalactic exchange.

Those natives whose karmic destiny it was to become spirit leaders of the time were patiently trained by the Yzhnüni as dedicated Keepers of the Crystals. The females of the race were perceived as receptive and nurturing, while the male vibration was seen to be better adapted to the peaceful pursuit of survival and the proliferation of the race, and so it was that those initiated in the Secret Wisdom were of the yin vibration.

Upon this fundamental understanding, the priestesses would later guide the natives in constructing their sacred stone circles and astronomical observatories, while continuing to perform individual and planetary balancing by connecting with other dimensions and planes. Those of the ancient Celtic Priesthood, the Druids, were carriers of this ancestral memory. We believe that you who are drawn to their mystical sites and sacred rituals are most likely to have been in body during the early epoch of the third cycle, resonating to Yzhnüni frequencies upon the great continent of Atlantis.

Such stone monuments, appearing there wherever the ancient Atlantean explorers passed, far outdate the estimates of your conservative archeologists. Indeed, the placing of gargantuan stones in the high grounds of South America, in Egypt, across the British Isles and Europe, in Mexico and the underwater city near Bimini, remains one of the great unsolved engineering mysteries of your time. It seems the academic establishment simply cannot determine how, why, when or by whom the great megalithic stones of temple sites, walls and burial grounds were constructed around the world and yet there they are–testimony to the greatness of what has come before you.

Still later generations of Atlantis would develop a keen awareness of the harnessing of crystal power for use in highly advanced technologies. Building upon the intuitive understanding of crystal energies handed down from the priestesses, as well as the environmental and sociological discoveries of the advancing culture, the Priesthood eventually guided the progress of society to reach a level of sophistication no less than yours. They, too, owed the basis of their technological prowess to the simple quartz crystal and they, too, built their technology around it.

Consider that the innate capabilities of *Homo Sapiens* are a constant throughout your existence; the DNA blueprint of your species is fundamentally identical. Although racial characteristics differ according to the original mixing of seed, only the evolutionary triggers and external influences affect the speed with which your race advances. If you look at the giant leaps in technology that you have taken in the last ten years, you should not find it inconceivable that over thousands of years the Atlanteans moved from crystal mountain healing caves to entire cities illuminated by underground crystal generators, programmed to capture human brain waves and transform them into 'electric' energy. This is a logical progression of your advancement, given the genetic resources of the human being, extraterrestrial intervention at key points in your evolution and the available resources on Planet Earth.

As you learn and experiment now with crystal energies, you are becoming ever more aware of how different minerals exhibit many subtle variations in their vibratory rates. Pure quartz, a hexagonal crystal matrix formed of silicon dioxide, is the ideal mineral for utilization in amplification, transfer and storage of all frequencies and emanations. It has forever been used throughout the galaxy for the transference of information, the light of wisdom and love, and still today it is the essential element of your electronic revolution. It is significant, relevant to the Atlantean paradigm, that modern Earth technology is dependent upon the infinitesimal microscopic sliver of quartz, which forms the microchip of your most extensive and sophisticated equipment.

In essence, without quartz, there most likely would never have been a technological revolution on Planet Earth. The caves of quartz crystal that abounded in Atlantis provided the Yzhnüni the ideal environment from which they would initiate the first Atlantean priestesses. They were trained to perform their healing ceremonies from within the caves, toning and balancing the individual by activating the elemental energies within the crystalline formations, while exalting the sonic and electromagnetic frequencies of the minerals themselves. The highly developed psychic abilities of earlier Atlanteans allowed them to hear the frequency, or wam vibration, as music.

Individuals who were no longer in harmony with their environment were brought to the caves, where the priestesses would tune in to their musical keyboard (the chakric system) to determine from which of the chakra centers were emanating the atonal frequencies.

Cushions of natural fibers (flax, woven reeds and animal furs) were lain over the crystal clusters; the seeker would then lie upon the amethyst healing bed, while the priestess, adept in the use of crystal energies, would strike the appropriate quartz formations with selenite tuning rods, activating the vibrational body and, in so doing, bringing the wam frequency of the individual back to resonance.

The use of sound in the healing and balancing of energy is incredibly powerful. Quite simply, the sound waves initiated with the striking of the appropriate crystalline structure activated the elemental energies within the matrix, which in turn resonated with the multidimensional frequencies of the individual seeking healing. A similar process can be affected by merely toning in the presence of a crystal being, and we cannot emphasize enough the magnitude of your united chanting, toning and laughter (music unto itself) when amplified through the minerals of Gaia. The priestess knowledge of crystalline frequencies determined the successful selection of the pitch, tone and frequency required to balance the chakric keyboard of the atonal one, and healing occurred spontaneously on many levels.

Their understanding of sound served not only to heal individuals in need of assistance; it was also understood to hold the entire planet in balance. Indeed, our knowledge of frequencies teaches us that it is sound that holds the body of All-That-Is together, the matrix into which light frequencies of consciousness are woven. Just as sound holds your planet in balance, discord can rip it apart. With this fundamental understanding of frequency, the Power that rules your modern world (like the Dark Priesthood of old) has Gaia teetering on the brink of dissolution.

The Dolphin Beings were introduced on Planet Earth to hold your oceans' sound frequencies in balance and for many millions of years they have performed that task with great eloquence. Only now, in the last nanosecond of Earth time, have they initiated their evacuation, and you are subsequently witnessing the breaking up of the seas with their systematic departure.

How could they have been expected to continue to serve Gaia when humans, the highest form of consciousness upon the Earth, have abused and violated her emotional body–the great oceans–with the stench of chemical dumping, raw sewage, petroleum spills and the total rape of the beings of the sea?

Forced into extinction, the Dolphin Beings, revered by the Atlanteans as the Weavers of the Ocean Frequencies, are finally leaving you. Their assignment has been invalidated by human neglect and indifference. This is a tragic development for your species and for your celestial body, whose music has been thrown off-key, just as it was then...in the late days of Atlantis, when the Dark Priesthood's manipulations destroyed forever the melody of Atlantis.

Once Earth played so harmoniously her song: the rhythmic ocean waves pounding upon the shores and roaring back out to sea; the melody of the winged creatures; the rustling of the winds; the articulated sounds of the Dolphin Beings; the chanting, chimes and drums of your native Keepers of the Frequencies; the chorus of human souls. Now she has become the loud, dissonant spinning wheel of your Sun's chakric body and it, too, must be attuned so that Ra can re-establish harmony throughout his mental-physical-emotional bodies.

Consider that Gaia, the communication chakra of your Solar Deity, is throwing the entire solar system out of key and you may recognize what an absolutely vital role sound and the understanding of sound frequencies are going to play in your future. You will understand, as well, how the Dark Priesthood of the Last Generation harnessed sound to control the elements and the beings of the continent and, in so doing, brought about its final destruction.

Drowning out the sounds of Gaia—emanating far into the upper atmosphere and out into space—are disturbing electromagnetic pulsations and destructive sound frequencies produced on Earth. From the hum of human noise to the reverberation from far too many satellites and electronic devices, they reach deep into Earth's auric field, rebounding through the material universe and rippling through simultaneous realities. You will need to address this aspect of your imbalance with urgency very soon. You will need to understand how sound, crystals and thought were made to interact then, with the submerging of a continent and now, with the revolution of the entire planet.

We elaborate on that crucial time of Atlantean development since the steady evolution of their crystal consciousness, so manipulated by the Dark Priesthood of the last generations, began there, many millennia before, in the light-filled caves of the Yzhnüni pioneers. Their intention in bringing the wisdom of the crystal beings to humanity was to gift you with their beauty and light, while awakening you to their utilization as vehicles for healing and attuning the mind-spirit and the body of the people and energies of Gaia. The dark use of crystals in the tools of technology, warfare and mind control devices came so much later that it is difficult to describe to you the great expanse of linear time that marks the 16,000 years to which we make reference here. It is extremely relevant to your contemporary Technological Age, which (in less than one hundred years) has reached almost similar proportions and, in the hands of the power elite managing Earth, threatens the same disastrous results.

We remind you, again and again, that in the extreme polarity of Earth consciousness, there are light and dark in all things, for this is the nature of polarity. You are constantly choosing...with every thought you send out and every action you take in your lives. Remember: you can be victimized only if you believe you are powerless. You can suffer the loss of your personal power only if you believe your soul can be taken from you. And you will fear death only if you remain ignorant to the process of the soul's evolution.

So it is in your contemporary world of modern technology and global communications, just as it is amongst those of you who are feeling tethered in the metaphysical pull between the light and the dark forces.

And so it was in the later generations of Atlantis.

# Chapter 6

# The Skull Committee

At a point in the Yzhnüni's earthly evolution, during which time they had effectively trained the novitiates in those practices that would help re-establish the wam frequencies of the natives and the entire ecosystem, the Sirian High Council intervened. We were intent upon accelerating the Atlanteans' understanding of multidimensionality and the higher purpose of humankind's existence, so that they would be able to carry on with the Yzhnüni's work of jump-starting the civilization's collective memory. It would connect them with the infinity of life streaming through the multi-dimensional body of All-That-Is.

It was our intention to ensure that the Yzhnüni's presence amongst your great ancestors serve to elevate the mutating starseeded human race from the bondage of survival mind into the pursuit of enlightenment, and to teach the Wisdom to those who would guide the people in that quest. We were directed to help dissolve the grid that had been made to envelop the Earth, so that we could re-establish direct lines of contact with you and with other life forms of your world.

To assist the noble Yzhnüni in their efforts, thirteen crystal skulls of extra-dimensional origins were brought into materialization, 'crystallized' in three-dimensional Earth frequencies much as you, as soul essences, create the physical bodies in which you reside as 3D beings. Remember that quartz crystals are living beings which record, store and amplify energy. You have seen this in their practical application in your technology and, although you may not quite understand how it works, you have accepted the use of the silicon chip as the foundation upon which that very technology is built.

Never forget, however, that throughout the universe of matter and permeating the infinite dimensions beyond your current 'slice' of reality, the capacity of crystal beings to serve consciousness is exalted when the matrix is activated by directed, focused thought waves of the few and the many. When that focus is set for the highest possible good of the All, magic happens.

As difficult as it might be for you to visualize or to accept, it is quite a simple process bringing crystal beings from an etheric imprint into matter, and this you may have already witnessed in your personal interactions with them. You may have experienced a crystal simply disappearing and then returning to you at another time or place. This is a phenomenon of universal scope and frequency and no, you aren't losing your mind if one of your crystal teachers seems to 'disappear into thin air'. It is just that the illusions of the world of matter may have you believing that such things cannot happen, just as you may believe that you, too, cannot disappear and return at will. Yet, such occurrences are reported frequently in those lands of ascetics and masters who achieve dematerialization as a result of what you term 'mind over matter'.

The thirteen skulls brought into manifestation in early Atlantis were 'sculpted' as a result of the mind-patterning of higher beings–members of the Family of Light–who were called from many dimensional frameworks to participate in their creation. Delivered unto the Earth realm by the Sirian High Council, they were programmed to open the portals of multi-dimensional awareness to the Yzhnüni...that they could continue their work with direct access to guidance from the higher dimensions. The thirteen skulls, known to the Family of Light as 'The Skull Committee', were stationed in the Temple of Nephthys, deep within an amethyst grotto in the inner earth sanctuary of Yzhnüni worship.

With our description of the temple, you may feel activation in the third eye center as your inner vision transforms the information into personal experience. You may feel inner guidance acknowledging this experience…remembering this 'place', for many of you know it on other levels and you have been holding the memory in your subconscious wells until this time of relevance. Similarly, you may project yourselves into that aspect of 'future', when the Skull Committee will be reunited at a predetermined site in the lands of the Maya.

You, of the early third cycle of Atlantis, can remember. We invite you to close your physical eyes, fold back the petals of Ajna, and see.

*"You are in a cavern lined in amethyst crystal clusters. Twelve crystal skulls have been stationed in a circular formation—the cosmometric configuration of All-That-Is—set to gaze upon the amethyst crystals which form the walls of the cave…they will activate the matrix at the appropriate time.*

*The thirteenth skull—the master—is held upon a spiral base of orichalcum in the circle's epicenter. It represents the seed…the consciousness of Prime Creator.*

*This is the entry point for the seers of Yzhnü for, through activation of the master, the twelve crystal skulls are brought to resonance, opening contact with other dimensions and the Light Ones of all frequencies…of worlds you had all but forgotten."*

Once the thirteen skulls had been activated, the interface between the Skull Committee and the Yzhnüni seekers served as a great galactic computer station, facilitating their on-going exchange with the Sirian High Council, the Galactic Federation, and higher dimensional beings throughout the Cosmos and across the no-time. All could be seen and heard in the boundlessness of All-That-Is, for it was a moment in three-dimensional time and space when the constraints had been removed. The Yzhnüni, who had finally learned to hold frequency in the world of matter, were once again free to travel to the far reaches of the Cosmos, in or out of their acquired three-dimensional forms.

It was intended that these most precious of all artifacts in your world be gifted to humanity long after the Yzhnüni left Earth's field, to serve as a perennial window upon the no-time for the Earth seers of the future. These gifts were to be handed down from the first priestesses to the Priesthood at a point in their awareness when they, too, would have reached mastery. As they peered through the multidimensional window, however, the Yzhnüni observed the perpetual (albeit infrequent) entry of Nebiru into your solar system. They observed the return of the Annunaki, their undermining of the Atlantean civilization and the disturbance they would eventually bring into the Priesthood. It was decided that it would be too dangerous to leave such power in their hands, for the eventual taking of the warriors of Anu.

The Yzhnüni knew the Nebiruans would be reintroducing technologies that would alter Earth's frequencies and create great disharmony amongst the populace. They realized that had they left the Skull Committee intact for the later generations of priests, the Annunaki would have eventually found a way to access the skulls. Masters of frequency, they could have manipulated the Priesthood to attempt a re-coding of the skulls, for purposes that were not of the highest order. Left in their hands, the Thirteen could have been utilized to retrieve information that would have served to perpetrate the Annunaki's advancing domination of your world, bringing even greater devastation to Earth and rippling out into the galaxy. By stimulating ego-centered consciousness in the Atlanteans, the Annunaki were actually setting the stage for the potential misuse of our greatest gift to you. This simply could not be allowed.

The Family of Light decreed that access to the Temple of Nephthys was to be forever denied the priestesses, and that much of the knowledge gleaned from the Skull Committee would have to be held in great secrecy for the remainder of the Yzhnüni's mission.

Before their departure from the Earth realm, they were instructed by the High Council to assign one of the twelve skulls to a select Keeper of the Crystals—one who had successfully completed initiation and had been deemed sufficiently disciplined in the mysteries and so pure in her intent that she could be entrusted with such monumental responsibility.

To each was assigned the solitary mission of carrying a skull in secrecy to a designated region of the Earth, there where the knowledge would eventually be reborn with its coming. This was the first exodus of the third cycle Atlanteans, more influential in the spreading of Atlantean wisdom that any wave of migration that would follow.

The Temple of Nephthys remained hidden in the underground of Atlán, despite the attempts of later generations of priests to discover the mythical site. It remained a vortex of such magnitude that the etheric imprint of the Committee held open a portal for thousands of Earth years–a galactic center that was later used as a point of entry into Earth's field by various forms of extra-planetary consciousness. Unfortunately, not all those who rode into that vortex were necessarily light beings. Never forget that polar forces exist on many planes, in varying degrees of intensity.

Although the Temple of Nephthys was drawn deep into the below of your world, beneath the sands of the Atlantic Ocean its crystalline form remains intact to this day. It remains one of the most powerful vortex points on your planet, where for countless decades ships and planes have vanished into the vapors. These mysterious events simply cannot be denied, for many official reports of the disappearance of military equipment, sea-faring craft and entire crews have described, with great detail, their vanishing from radar controls from one second to another: a scientific 'impossibility'.

Ironic, isn't it? While your mechanical, logical world refutes spiritualists' claims of dematerialization, attempting to de-bunk all evidence of such experience amongst you, radar equipment confirms entire aircraft and great ships 'here and gone' in an instant from the seas and airspace of the vortex zone. Surely, if such enormous vessels can dissipate into the ethers, then the appearance and disappearance of extra-dimensional crystal skulls in three-dimensional reality should not be too terribly difficult to incorporate into that body of thought which you consider 'plausible'.

We wish to reiterate that, although the thirteen crystal skulls were removed from the amethyst Temple of Nephthys, it is still **operative**. What has been imprinted in the energy fields of the sacred grotto has created a sort of multidimensional tunnel, where matter escapes into parallel realities just as other forms of consciousness crystallize in 3D, and it is due to resurface at the time of your progression into the fourth dimension. Many changes in the terrain will take place from now until the shifting, and of this you are well aware, as increasingly high-force earthquakes shake and re-position your lands and the volcanoes extend and mould the landscape. Much of the underground will come to surface, while other points will sink into the below and this is representative of Gaia's shifting consciousness and emotional assessments...her relinquishing of form as she prepares to move into light body.

Of the fate of the skulls, the master was deemed too powerful for human hands. It was de-materialized and re-assigned to the sixth dimension for safekeeping, until a time when the Committee would be reunited upon Earth to serve in the Great Work that was seen to lie ahead for humanity. It was foreseen that the Keepers of the Crystals would return, revealing themselves to each other and then joining together to re-open the window of the Cosmos for the instruction and preparation of those who would be moving with Gaia into the fourth dimension.

These are very old souls...the reincarnated Keepers now holding body amongst you...and theirs is a sacred task. They have come into the incarnation to reunite the Thirteen just before the closing of the year 2012 when, as part of Earth's process of shifting, the galactic computer station will again be needed by the light forces of Gaia. This could not have occurred until your male-driven civilization, having passed apex point and then having exacerbated the subsequent phase of self-destruction, began to once again resonate to the yin vibration.

This, the return of the pendulum, has begun with the Age of Aquarius.

*         *         *

You reached apex point at mid-century, with the explosion of the atomic bomb in the lands of Nippon. That explosion sent a shiver through the body of All-That-Is, and all the conscious beings of the Universe who felt its intense vibration realized that Gaia, the Garden of Eden, would never be the same again. With that irresponsible act, the governments of Earth completely lost their focus. The aggressive force was imposed on you like a false god, sold to you as the only way to defend and honor your nations...of protecting yourselves from the 'others'. You, the human race, entered the phase of the breaking down of your beliefs, your creations and your dreams of utopia. The mass mind stopped caring about the animals, the seas and the garden and lost its spirit. Not even in Atlantis, in those dark days of the Last Generation, did humanity reach such a state of total alienation.

Those beyond your world—we, who watch events unfolding in the Cosmos—shuddered, knowing what would follow. This vile action against the Living Earth, the detonating of such a colossal, destructive force, was presented to humanity as a deterrent against evil...but that was sheer camouflage and, moreover, it was **overkill** in every sense of the word. Rather, the great explosion was meant as a message to the world from the Management Team, those we have defined as the Secret Government. They were letting you know unequivocally that, from that point on, they held absolute power over you and that they could, at will, destroy all life on your planet. Never forget that the leaders of the political alliance that still claims title as the United Nations for Peace were those who dropped the bombs of destruction. This act of irreverent omnipotence was committed under the guise of 'establishing the peace', but what was actually being imposed upon you was a new reign of power that was to forever rule the Earth.

The great explosion provided the impetus for the power elite to drive you into separation, creating a fundamental belief structure that would convince you of your righteousness as nations (and, subsequently, as individuals) intent upon upholding the laws of survival...justifying all violence against the 'enemy'. It set the example for the future of Earth–domination by force–and you sensed how your lives had become forever fragile and tenuous from that moment on.

It should not surprise you that a time of untold violence and rage has followed that act, a plague that has brought you to fear for the very future of Planet Earth. In the last fifty years, you have witnessed society breaking down its ethics, its spirit and its values…and with that, such destruction. This is simply part of the curve leading to the awakening of the nurturing female–your yin selves. From the pain and tragedy of human violence and the disruption of the ecosystems, you are moving now to be healed in the Great Mother's embrace.

You have reached the time of neutralizing the destructive force, and the light of dawn is awakening you from your troubled sleep. Very soon now you will have evolved to a point as the body of consciousness of Gaia when the Thirteen will reappear and the window will be re-opened. We are aware of many man-made effigies being discovered at this time, crystal skulls that have been unearthed from key sites in the lands of the Maya and they are powerful, holding the records of their ancient keepers. But of the crystal skulls that have come into public awareness, only three held the portal in the Temple of Nephthys.

Of those still to be brought to the foreground, one is in the hands of Tibetan Elders; others are held by Keepers in select tribes of the Americas; one lies buried beneath the sea; another below the sands of the Sahara; others are cloaked in total secrecy or still buried in the cool of the earth. This is as it was meant to be. The time is almost upon you when all will surface and the Skull Committee will be reunited. The master will once again materialize at the reunion, which is scheduled to occur in the lands of the Maya, directed by the Mayan teachers of time, for they are the key players here.

What is important is that the skulls be brought together at the appointed hour in their resonant vibratory fields. This has been arranged. It has been programmed within the skulls and we are working now to facilitate the coming together of the Keepers, as was ordained at the beginning of the third cycle of Atlantis.

It may seem incredibly fantastic to you—a collective of thirteen crystal skulls opening the Cosmos to the Yzhnüni seers in Atlantis—or even more implausible that you are about to experience that portal opening again. But then…is it that much different than, say, the expansive galactic vision provided by the command station of NASA's space launch control center? We ask you. Would gazing into a complex 21st century computer system by one who has only known life in the deepest jungles of Brazil or the remote deserts of the Sahara—your contemporaries—be any more incredible than the idea of crystal skulls as viewing machines of the Universe is to you?

Retrace your steps. You will find reference to the skulls everywhere, for we were sure to leave you the signs. Observe the Aztec stone calendar, inherited from the Olmecs and the Mayan Keepers of the Records. Carved at the center of the circular time map is the depiction of a skull, testimony of their astute understanding of time: the cyclical nature of time in your dimension and the recognition of the no-time that lay beyond. They, Keepers of three skulls of the Committee, were able to see into the 'future' and into the 'past'. They had achieved awareness of the fact that your Solar Deity would be moving beyond time, past what they understood to be the fifth and final Sun.

The placing of the skull's image in the center of the calendar was representative of the Mayan understanding that the closing of time was to herald Gaia's passage into the no-time/all-time of multidimensional consciousness and an end to Earth's perpetual rebirthing in the realm of matter. It was a prophesy of hope rather than doom, a vision of a new beginning for a world that would be reaching the end of a way of being. Or rather, the end of a way of perceiving. The end of time.

How better to record the 'future' events of your Sun's ascension—the passing from the three-dimensional constraints of your reality—than by placing the figure of the skull, the cosmic computer of the no-time, at the absolute center of the calendar record? Like the great vortex into whose center you are now gravitating for your passage into the fourth dimension, the skull, at the center of the Mayan calendar, represents the opening of Earth consciousness to the higher states of timeless awareness and limitless experience. Moreover, the central skull carving was meant to foretell of a point when, with the closing of the record (the end of time as you have known it in 3D), the master skull would be returned to activate the Committee.

Skull carvings exist at many temple complexes, particularly in Tibet, Peru, the lands of the Maya and other strategic locations reached by the third cycle Atlanteans who followed the priestesses in their migrations away from the mainland, establishing the ancient knowledge for future generations to carry forth. It was not a difficult undertaking, considering the breadth of the continent, which stretched from as far north as Iceland down to the land mass known to you as South America. Migration from the great continent was absolutely natural, almost like skipping over polished stones in a riverbed to reach the banks at the other side.

That is how the Wisdom and the legend of the Skull Committee spread across your globe. It is how the Yzhnüni bequeathed to the many civilizations that would follow the disaster brought on by the Dark Atlantean Priesthood the wisdom that the light would return to your world, and that the dawn of planetary ascension was recognizable in linear time. The natives, Keepers of the Records, knew. They were entrusted with the memory.

*        *        *

The power elite are remotely aware of the crystal skulls, although they cannot imagine their immensity and scope because they simply do not find resonance with them from the narrow band of emotional and mental body frequencies in which they operate. Nonetheless, they have long attempted to sabotage any ancestral memory of the Skull Committee by distorting the image of the skull in your minds, creating associations that provoke fear within you: pictures of pirates' flags, poisonous concoctions, deadly currents and Halloween ghouls. These configurations of the skull's effigy have been drawn for you deliberately, for the Power has not wanted you to retrieve this memory. They were warned that the reuniting of the skulls would once again provide the human race with access to the higher realms, just as they knew that the programming of the Skull Committee had been set to keep them from accessing them. They knew it would be useless to even attempt it, so they have not bothered to pursue the Keepers or take what could never be theirs from you.

Convinced, as they are, that they are the absolute masters of technology, the power elite cannot really imagine a source superior to theirs. They are, unquestionably, privy to some highly impressive technologies, of which you still have seen very little manifest in society. Much is secret, being held from you for their own covert activities and their advancement, and simply because most of it is designed to control you. They love that. They love believing that you, the entire human race, are their subjects and that lording the technology over you will keep you in submission.

What do they think of the possibility that you could soon be given back a window on the no-time? Surely the management team does not want you actually 'observing' what they can only project into the future. Why then, you might ask, are they so disinterested in the skulls?

Know that the management philosophy of the Annunaki has always been based upon a three-fold principle: the manipulating of your thoughts; the stimulation of your ego selves; the shutting down of your heart centers. If the propaganda is effective, and you believe skulls to be symbols of evil and death, you simply will not be drawn to them and they believe that this has been effective enough to deflect your interest. They are so convinced of their superiority over you and are so absorbed in their own doings that they are not particularly concerned about your bringing the Thirteen together in time for the shift. They simply aren't focused on that possibility because they believe that they have disempowered you...that the reuniting of the Skull

Committee is more the wishful thinking of a few superstitious natives than it is the keyhole of your liberation.

By taking the indigenous peoples from their lands and reassigning them to settlements, camps and reservations, they have intentionally set out to break the consciousness of place and being that has held the frequency in the sacred sites. They believe they have disarmed you completely by uprooting the Keepers of Frequency and sending the Keepers of the Crystals into hiding. And yet, despite the Power's efforts to silence the voice of the native peoples of your world, they are surfacing now as the guides who will help lead you into the New World. They have held alive their knowledge of the Fifth Sun and are coming into center stage, now that you are opening enough to hear their message.

There is another aspect that calls for your consideration. At a time when the power elite are looking for a desperate way out of the mess they have created and the Annunaki are lost out in galactic night with no apparent way back in time for ascension, they may just welcome whatever insights you can gather by opening a portal. At a point when all seems to be lost in the game and they recognize that their hold over you is about to end in a total shift in Earth's complex body, they surely would gravitate to any additional visions and knowledge that might come to you from higher sources. Theirs is a passive involvement. They are observing you, awaiting the results of your lightworking, believing they can somehow let you tap into source and then steal the wisdom for their own needs and intentions.

Let that not concern you. Theirs are acts of desperation, whereas yours are of love and celebration.

Just as the control tower of Cape Canaveral looks out upon the universe of matter, so the Skull Committee will provide you, the Light Ones of Gaia, with a cosmic overview of the no-time, as it did in Atlantis. This will help you anchor the light at a time when great waves of fear will be rolling through the masses, for things are becoming very difficult for you now, as you begin to feel the pull of your reality slipping out of the third dimension.

You will be called upon to chart and guide Gaia's passage through the vortex by holding consciousness in the love center. You must be cleared of all miasmic patterns that you have held as race memory from the time of the Annunaki's invasion, from as far back as the execution of the Great Experiment.

The Keepers of the Crystal Skulls are waiting for a specific sign. This is held secret amongst them, but it was foreseen by the first Keepers of the Crystals and passed down. Celestial events are already performing a sort of dance from which you can glean the next steps. The total solar eclipse of the closing millennium marked your full-scale progression towards the vortex and served to draw your attention upward, making you aware of the changes that are taking place at the macrocosmic level. The aligning of nine planetary bodies of your Solar Deity at the onset of the new millennium marks yet another preparatory event, for it is like a dress rehearsal of what will be required at the time of passing.

There will be a distinct and unmistakable sign from the heavens when all will move into the final stages; this will take form as a sort of solar flare that seems to burn in the skies. It will be experienced as a third eye vision by the Keepers of the Crystal Skulls and soon thereafter the discoveries will be forthcoming.

The hidden will soon come out of hiding; preparations for the great reunion are already underway. You are being guided by the Family of Light.

# Chapter 7

## Thought Waves and the Collective Mind

It is essential that we clarify and define our terms, if we are to succeed in making clear to you just how thought can be evoked, stimulated and manipulated by various mechanisms within as well as outside of you. The fundamental process of mental exchange–the transmitting and receiving of thought waves–forms the basis upon which you can develop an understanding of the Atlantean paradigm. That is why being aware of these aspects of human consciousness has never been more important to you than it is now, in the pre-dawn hours of your ascension.

The Universe of God is a thriving, vibrant totality of consciousness and all its elements are alive and constantly transmuting into new states of being. Nothing is dead or static in the cosmic body of All-That-Is. There is simply an infinite range of vibration to which every aspect, from the immensity of a galaxy to the inconceivably minute subatomic particle, holds resonance. The Cosmos of soul is pure energy, an electromagnetic being of traversing, interpenetrating waves which, by their nature, reflect the dual personality of Prime Creator: the electric, outward-moving yang force and the magnetic, receptive yin vibration. The dynamic of these interacting energies, the yin/yang relationship, is the nature of all things–at all levels of existence. It is procreation, dissolution, vibration, harmony and contrast; it is the very structure of the frequencies of the Universe.

This electromagnetic energy, the conscious manifestation of All-That-Is, moves in waves exhibiting both electric and magnetic properties, crests and troughs of varying breadth, velocity and pitch, and these aspects are measurable (from a limited 3D spectrum) in earthly terms.

In your lexicon, the **wave length** describes the distance between waves. **Frequency** indicates the number of waves occurring in a sixty-second time frame and can be described as the cycle, or pulse, of the wave pattern. This measure is known in your existing terminology by the name **Hertz**. Variations in these two aspects create the vast range of electromagnetic waves which fill the Universe: from slowly oscillating radio waves to the rapidly vibrating cosmic rays at the high end of the spectrum and beyond. All is infinite and there are immeasurable frequencies of the Godself which defy definition.

The human brain operates within a specific range of electromagnetic frequencies, and these we would describe as 'thought waves', while your scientists prefer to use the term, 'brain waves'. Ironically, chemical testing and the recording of brain wave activity form the basis of your medical research into the workings of the human mind, yet most of the main-stream still denies the existence of telepathic communication, relegating such basic employment of resonant wave frequencies as metaphysical mumbo-jumbo—publicly, that is. Privately, the governments of power have invested elaborate funding and substantial effort training high-ranking military and intelligence officers in the study and practice of telepathic communication, thought implantation and remote viewing—three forms of brain wave link-up. This is very much a part of your reality now as it was then, in the days of dark Atlantis.

In keeping with the concept of the simple measuring of brain wave activity, we wish to reiterate that telepathy is a gift you all enjoy at some level. It is high time that humanity recognize these innate capacities as standard operating equipment of the species, for there is nothing super-natural about thought traversing the space between you. You simply catch the wave and ride it in. Much like the tuning of a radio dial to obtain a clear channel, you reach each other by finding the 'transmitting station' of the other and tuning in to that station's frequency. Some are more adept than others; some train and work at developing this ability, but all conscious beings, units of the All-That-Is, have the capacity to receive and send thought waves through the ethers. You do it all the time, communicating on many levels.

After being synchronized to Sirian frequencies in the Hyper-dimensional Spiral, our instrument has been attuned to operate as a receptive channel for six-dimensional transmitters and that, again, is a simple demonstration of how consciousness traverses the cosmic sea. By establishing resonance, we communicate...plain and simple. Attuning interdimensionally is, in a certain sense, more complex than connecting with those of your same realm; in other ways it is far more simple. The 'lines' are clearest at 04:00, the violet hour of Gaia, when the least amount of electromagnetic interference exists and Trydjya is most receptive. It is for this reason that we rouse her from her sleep, although as her abilities become keener, we are finding greater time spans in which to transmit. It is a matter of frequency and resonance, the basis of which is purely scientific. In Sirian terms, we would describe our connection to her as being 'cosmometrically proportional'.

What is important here is that you recognize how energy in motion has no borders, boundaries or limitations. Basically, all that is required for an individual to receive or send transmission is the establishing of the elements of resonance with another form of consciousness.

You are not encouraged to believe that you 'hear' messages–neither those passing between you nor those being beamed in from other dimensions. Yet, governments have been performing experiments in this field for decades, developing sophisticated and quite sinister applications of their acquired knowledge for uses that control and manipulate the minds of those targeted by the technology. You would be surprised to learn how many of the classified 'psychopaths' imprisoned in your

mental institutions are merely hearing the thoughts of telepathic transmitters who are sending from various levels of consciousness. Of these,
significant numbers are the test cases of your own governments' experi-
menting in the fields of mental manipulation.

It is important that you understand how the brain transmits and
receives information, so that you can comprehend how you contribute to
the whole with your thoughts, affecting interpersonal and global vibrations, and how others contribute to yours. Similarly, it is becoming
extremely important to recognize how vast numbers of people can be
entrained and manipulated at subliminal levels by those who surf your
thought waves and reach resonance with you. Therefore, we feel it necessary to provide an elementary explanation of the workings of the mind,
for it is with your minds that we are connecting here, in these written
manifestations of inter-dimensional thought transference, as they have
been interpreted, decoded and recorded by our instrument, Trydjya.

You, the readers, are actually no less connected to us than she; all is
fluid and pulsating between us. As you allow the words to enter into your
minds, you are responding on many levels, experiencing chemical reactions in your neural networks.

Four basic groups of brain wave frequencies identify the predominant
categories of mental activity:

| | |
|---|---|
| Beta Waves | (13-35 pulses per second) |
| Alpha Waves | (8-12 pulses per second) |
| Theta Waves | (4-7 pulses per second) |
| Delta Waves | (.5-3 pulses per second) |

Medical and scientific researchers have established that beta waves are
registered when an individual's mental activity is conscious, active and
alert. States of anxiety and agitation cause the brain to emit frequencies at
the high end of that range: these are shorter, more rapid wave frequencies.
Those which you refer to as 'alpha waves' are frequencies of the human
brain in states of calm and relaxation, what we would like to call the

'receptive mind'. Stilling the mind even further, one vibrates in theta, where psychic vision, past life memory, dreams and astral visions are experienced. Finally, the long, slow delta waves are recorded in deep sleep, there where **seemingly** very little brain activity is occurring.

Studies of the human electronics board–the neural networks–involve understanding how these varying frequencies refuel neurochemicals within the body, and how that function sets up reactions in the brain, which then manifest as mental, emotional and physical responses. Given what we have told you of resonance and the interacting of thought, sound and light waves, is it so difficult to imagine how certain 'influences' can be imposed upon the wave frequencies of another to deliberately alter his/her mental, emotional or physical states of being?

Factors of influence over the human mind are constantly being used for both the dark and light intention. Consider how, when you join together in deep meditation, guided by one whose light, loving presence amongst you serves to set the alpha or theta wave frequency, the entire group can be entrained to that state of mind by reaching resonance with that vibration. Simplified, it would be as if the guide were acting as a sort of mental metronome, establishing the frequency to which the others become attuned. It is not difficult to understand how joining in such pleasant unions leaves you feeling connected and harmonious with the members of the group, for you reach each other at the same frequency and similar neurochemical responses occur within all of you. If the group's intention is to radiate outwards the light of love within you, all will feel the wonder of that evocation pulsing between you...at the same frequency. You experience the waves of the Godlight amplified between you–the Oneness–and that is a most superb aspect of entrainment.

You can imagine how enough lightworkers praying and working together to raise the vibration of the greater environment can affect larger numbers of the populace, as those group waves of light and love become the beacons for others who are struggling in the darkness of their anxiety, fear and disharmony. If enough of you unite for the light, the power of your thoughts will resonate with Gaia's own electromagnetic frequencies for she, too, is emanating consciousness in undulating waves of pure energy. The Gaian pulse is sent out across the body of your Solar Deity and on to the far reaches of the galaxy. The heart of the Goddess beats the rhythm.

You can see why we are forever reminding you how your every thought affects the entirety, and why it is so absolutely important that each of you learn to stay centered, calm and peaceful in the wake of the changes are taking place around you. Your centeredness, you understand, resonates as a certain frequency that moves upon the cosmic sea as waves, and those very waves can be 'surfed' by those around you. Connecting with each other in this way, you sense the energies of the other there, out on the oceans of cosmic mind. You spread the light of love out onto other dimensions and other planes, there where the Light Ones of many worlds experience the radiance of your heartsong. You create a peaceful, harmonious reality, where all is in balance and that vibration extends endlessly outward to the heavens and inward, down to the very subatomic particles which form the basic structure of your being.

But what if the vibrational pace-setter were of the dark intention? Suppose one or more individuals, who would control others for personal or political gain, were intent upon imposing some form of mental interference that would set up another form of entrainment: a pre-determined frequency intended to create certain desired chemical changes to occur within the receiver? As there is light...so is there darkness. It should not surprise you to think that knowledge of the brain's functions and the mind's susceptibility are just as available to those who prefer to linger in the shadows and they, too, can affect desired reactions by reaching resonance with others. What if one were to introduce an external element which would stimulate within your brain responses of extreme angst and frustration...of rage, or terror...and hold you there, resonating to that current, in a constant state of disharmony and fear?

We assure you that entrainment of large sectors of the population has always occurred on your planet: the Light Ones radiating love on your frequency bands; the dark ones reaching you through fear and ignorance. Covert mind games were as much a tool of the Dark Priesthood of Atlantis as they are of the 21st century Secret Government. Known as 'mind manipulation warfare', this subversive aspect of mind control is a very real development in military research. Indeed, governments have become much more overt in its application since the first detonation of the atomic bomb–when they affirmed their total power over all life in your world and stopped worrying too terribly much about how humankind would respond to their expressions of omnipotence.

Let us say that if you want to acquire more specific information regarding the potential applications of mind manipulation technology, much material has become available. Books and detailed reports have been written by the bold amongst you who dare to question the authority...but tread lightly, for this is a dangerous area for the inquisitive. **You are not supposed to ask these questions.**

*             *          *          *

One of the most cost-effective ways to alter human brain activity and stimulate neurochemical reactions at the group level is through the use of inaudible electromagnetic pulsations–extremely low frequency waves–that can be transmitted by beaming specific frequencies at certain target areas. You may remember a brief appearance in the media of a story regarding Russian emissions of a low-frequency radio signal, which was being secretly beamed at the American Embassy in that country's capital. Referred to as the 'Woodpecker', this frequency was carried in like an ocean wave carries in its wake various particles and elements from the sea.

We suggest here that hidden in the peaks and valleys of any wave formation can exist other aspects which can catch the wave, so to speak, and ride in undetected. A disruptive electromagnetic pulse, hidden in the wave band of an innocuous emission, could so be transmitted and received at the mental level. This invasive technology was still unknown to U.S. intelligence at the time of its employment in Russia. Although the American agents were suspicious of some form of external interference, they simply didn't know what they were looking for or how to intercept at the correct frequency level.

In fact, many employees of the embassy reported suffering various degrees of discomfort and emotional stress, but for a while no one could understand what was causing so many staff members to fall ill. It took a while for the Americans to discover that a disruptive agent was being beamed into their brains, causing chemical reactions in the neurons, which were then triggering mental, emotional and physical responses within them.

The Soviets knew what they were doing; they understood that certain electromagnetic emissions can alter human states of health and harmony. Interfering with the natural pulse of Earth, your home resonating board, can simply change the internal musical keyboard and create dissonance on all levels. It can flip the chakric system; disturb body rhythms; evoke neurochemical reactions in the brain and alter the very DNA within you. These, dear ones, are the primary intentions of electromagnetic controls on Planet Earth.

Woodpecker, the Soviet's once-secret weapon, is yesterday's news, paling in comparison to what is being developed now—yet, it is the fundamental expression of mind manipulation technology. If you wish to investigate further, you can begin by exploring media reports from the 1970s to find validating information of the Woodpecker Affair. You may also uncover other mood manipulation technologies being tested on animals and humans alike...in the name of 'science'. It is happening all around you. The story is buried in the archives, but you can bring it to the surface if you are willing to dig through the camouflage.

Beware of searching for such controversial information on the Internet, exposing yourselves in ways that will not be in your best interest. You must be discerning when investigating the affairs of the power elite, recognizing the danger zones. Different roads often lead to the same destination.

*　　　　*　　　　*

Disturbing electromagnetic frequencies, subliminal sounds and other forms of mind manipulation were imposed upon the noble people of Atlantis at the time the Priesthood polarized into dark and light forces and–aided by the Annunaki–the cloaked ones set out to take control of the population. There were many layers of intent involved: from the projections of the intervening Annunaki, to the ambitions of those priests who chose to operate from ego-centered consciousness. We ask you to bear in mind that this was a gradual process and it was subtle…so much so that the people were completely unaware of the shifting social design until it was far too late to alter the outcome.

At an earlier time during the third cycle of Atlantis, well before the dark forces intervened there, the citizenry began to organize into complex communal structures, much like those of your modern world. They created laws and selected governmental leaders, established trade and commercial exchange within and beyond their borders, determined acceptable social behaviors, and practiced elaborate spiritual rituals.

Like so many civilizations that followed, most of their prayer and worship was dedicated to Ra, the Ra-diant One, your Solar Deity. It has been this way throughout Earth time, for as starseed you have always looked to the Sun as the source of life and abundance. Ra has been the most celebrated deity of Earth's entire history, just as it has been that of other civilizations still outside of your conscious reference. Ancient earth temples all face east, as did those of Atlantis, in anticipation of Ra's appearance upon the horizon, for the ancients were far more attuned than you are now.

Every new dawn was a reaffirmation of life and connection to the Solar Deity. Nightfall was always a time of quiet reflection and waiting, of gazing out to the suns of other realms and wondering…for some, remembering.

The High Priesthood, descendants of the priestesses of early Atlantis, slowly formed a governing order, a body of leadership which addressed the spiritual and practical needs of the society. Prayer was required; the priests called their subjects to worship at four distinct intervals throughout the daily cycle: sunrise, midday, sunset and midnight. These solar aspects were considered: the emergence of Ra; the full light of the Solar Deity; the retreat of Ra; the awaiting of the return of the Divine Light.

With their ancestral understanding of the nature of crystals (taught by the legendary Yzhnüni Crystal Beings and handed down over the millennia) and the abundance of minerals that existed upon that continent, it was only natural that the Atlanteans incorporate crystals into their meditations and rituals. With time and practice they learned to recognize the subtle reality shifts that occurred when prayer was called; they grew to appreciate how crystals amplified their thoughts and illuminated their states of reverence. As their experience intensified, they reached an understanding of just how a desired material outcome could be physically manifested via the mental power of One Mind.

In the short time frame that resembles your own leap from candles to lasers, they had developed the technology which we have consistently referred to as the 'mindlight generators'. A system of these underground crystal energy stations existed in all populated centers across the continent. They are the mechanisms witnessed in the dreamtime of our instrument, referred to in her earlier writings as the 'recurring dream'.

Each crystal tower consisted of a large pyramidal or cone-like coil structured of orichalcum, upon which immense quartz spheres were positioned. Quartz, the fundamental component with which the human mind would interact, was grown in laboratory conditions so that the specimens used in the generators would be of the purest quality. During this process, gold filaments formed in the shape that you know as the yod (the fundamental form of the Hebrew alphabet) were imbedded in each growing crystal matrix. They served as conduits for the process of mind-link amongst the collective, just as that sacred form continues to serve scholars as a link to Divine Mind in the ancient written records of the Hebrew texts.

Activation of the mindlight generators involved an obligatory ritual which was performed daily at morning ritual–the Emergence of Ra. It centered around a visualization meditation of the population-at-large, whereby all citizens of Atlantis were guided to focus and project their thoughts into the generators, with the specific intention of storing and amplifying the electromagnetic frequencies of the collective and transmuting that source into a form of physical energy. This process further involved connecting to Gaia, achieving a level of resonance that would draw powerful surges of energy up through the coils to unite with the collective mind.

This process manifested as 'illumination' on many levels. The free energy provided was of such abundance that the Atlanteans never needed to disturb the resources of the rich earth; never did they create waste-producing power plants or harm the environment. No tree was felled, no sea or ocean contaminated; the deep inner body of Earth was left intact. Moreover, never was the source of the interactive energies of Earth and its beings the 'property' of the few, for it was the All who manifested it and to the All it was provided.

As the influences of the dark side began to take seed in the Priesthood, however, the idyllic era of unity began its shift into a time of separation and ego consciousness. Individuals of the higher ranks recognized the personal gains that could be won in such an environment and the intervention of the Annunaki at that time consolidated their behavior. Rewards were reaped by those who served the Power. Emphasis was placed on the needs of the individual and personal desire was stimulated so that, before long, the One Heart became but a legend of ancestral claim.

\*   \*   \*

By now, we believe we have made it clear to you that the Annunaki, warriors of Nebiru, require enormous amounts of energy to survive their endless journey through the galactic winter, and that their primary source of that energy is supplied by Planet Earth.

This fact has had enormous repercussions upon Earth reality for many hundreds of thousands of years. Their return during the Last Generation was particularly fruitful, for they found a civilization that had surpassed the tedium of mining Earth's resources and which had learned, instead, to tap Gaia's abundant energy through the power of the human mind. Their observations of Atlantis convinced them that developments in human consciousness had reached such a point that they could easily take over Planet Earth. They perceived the Atlantean civilization as the perfect blueprint from which plans could be designed to encircle the globe, whereby all conscious beings upon the planet could eventually be manipulated to serve their needs and to provide them with unlimited energy. They anticipated that, by imposing mind manipulation technologies within these structures to 'use' the mind and soul of Gaia and the human race, they would eventually achieve that end.

The Dark Priesthood grew in number and in strength; the pendulum swung to the dark side. Like modern day experimenters in brain wave modification technology, alchemists of their time were instructed to experiment with the source of this energy: the collective mind of the citizens of Atlantis. They were to find ways to amplify dramatically the capabilities of the crystal generators, but first they had to manipulate the population into performing for the private interests of the Power. No longer an act of love and community, the ritual of energizing the generators became one of obedience and duty.

Their method involved the transmitting of a very slow electromagnetic pulse through the crystal generator networks traversing the key cities of the continent. This subliminal sound, inaudible to the human ear, stimulated neurochemical reactions causing irrational mental states, predominantly of **submission.** Like the Woodpecker of the Soviets so many thousands of years later, the insipid traveler surfed (unidentified) the brain waves of the collective Atlantean mind.

You are well aware of the effect a steady drop of water in a silent room can have upon the human psyche. This form of mental torture has been utilized in recent cultures as a form of punishment, eventually leading to insanity in the subjected victim. It should not surprise you that a similar use of inaudible pulses has existed from as far back as Atlantis, or that it is once again being utilized today. You have only to explore the information that is available to you and tune in to what is going on around you. Opening your minds, your ears and eyes, you cannot help but understand…just as many of you will **remember.**

Consider that Gaia, too, has her natural frequency, one that resonates with all life forms within and upon her body. Raising your awareness to one of global proportions, isn't it just possible that manipulating frequencies might in the same way be deliberately imposed upon her inner body, throwing her out of balance as well? Is it too far beyond reason to believe that this is already happening…so far fetched that you can only consider it 'science fiction'? Then we ask you. What could be more ethically inconceivable than your governments' continuous explosion of atomic warheads in your seas, sold to you as the testing of various nuclear arsenals (as if one bomb's success assures another's) in the name of 'national defense'? Or the systematic killing of the Dolphin Beings and Great Whales, Weavers of the Frequencies of the oceans? And of the satellites that are proliferating in Earth's outer body, what do you know?

Do you wonder if there, too, disturbances of Gaia's frequencies are being deliberately created to hold the entire planet in imbalance? There are electromagnetic frequencies coming at you through the Internet as well, entraining you, and this is experienced by many as feeling 'hooked' by the technology. As diabolical as it all sounds, de-stabilizing Earth and its life forms is, in large part, deliberate. It is all part of the master plan. Would you still worship and obey your leaders if there were no strife or crises from which to be saved?

We perceive as a total paradox the destroying of Gaia as a natural result of human advancement. It simply does not equate. And yet global devastation is your reality as you spin into the new millennium, swirling into the vortex. Therefore, do not be so skeptical as to refuse to believe that those same governments are currently sending shock waves into the earth to deliberately trigger earthquakes, tidal waves and ecological disasters for reasons that reflect the lower vibration of those who hold the power.

One is the knowledge that they must lighten the load of Gaia, and so masses of people must be eliminated. Another is their intention to control the planet's electromagnetic frequencies, for reasons that we will elaborate in our next transmission. Yet another is their desire to keep you in fear and survival mode so that you remain separate and enslaved, bowing down to the secret masters: the power elite, their earthly descendants.

Above all else, however, is the Power's determination to harness the geophysical forces of the planet and to utilize that awesome energy in an exercise that will be nothing more than a replay of the Atlantean Error.

Much of the devastation that surrounds you results from their foolish manipulation of earth energies, for they are always looking for ways to harness Gaia for their own interests. In their short-sighted vision of wealth, power and control they have blasted, burned, poisoned, bored and chiseled away at the body of Gaia relentlessly...taking, taking, taking. They have encased the Earth in cement, suffocating the life force from her. They have embroiled you in their nets, entrained you, manipulating your thoughts and emotions by holding your animal selves in their vibrational cages.

And now, when one would hope that they might just recognize in the disastrous unfolding of events the no-win scenario of such doings, they have created **HAARP.**

# Chapter 8

## HAARP and Earth's Auric Field

Consider what we have told you about resonance and thought waves and let us now expand the concept to one which would be intent upon actually measuring and synchronizing with the fundamental vibrations of Earth–the idea of reaching resonance with your planet deity as an **entirety**. She, too, vibrates at specific frequencies, creating chemical reactions within her 'neurons' and she, too, responds and interacts with the collective mind of Earth beings and with her sister deities in the Cosmos. Bear in mind that all conscious beings upon, within and above the Earth are reflections of that vibration, just as every cell within your body is a reflection of yours…as every subatomic particle reflects the cell and on and on…throughout infinity.

Following that line of 'cosmic' reasoning, it should appear plausible to you that if one can achieve resonance at such an unfathomable vibrational level, the very essence of Earth's physical being can be potentially altered or manipulated to serve some specific purpose. This would have to mean that every live element and biological component of Earth (reflections of the greater body) would then be equally affected…and that is indeed the case.

We shall use as an example a simple wine glass…the 'chalice'. Running a finger around its outer rim will activate the consciousness–or energy–within the glass, affecting a reaction at the subatomic level. Applying the correct formula of pressure, velocity and conscious thought (intent) to the action, one can cause the chalice to emit a sound (an electromagnetic frequency) which reflects its relative proportions, density and dimensions: its physical nature. Insisting, one might achieve the right vibration (that which we intend as 'resonant' with the physical properties of the glass) which could actually cause the chalice to explode or shatter to bits...altering the form of its existence in physical matter.

Physicists can explain in scientific terms how sound produced by sustained vibrational frequency can cause a seemingly fixed structure to alter form. Through your observation of the workings of energy, you do know this to be true, yet the idea somehow challenges your core beliefs regarding the nature of matter, particularly that which you believe to be 'non-living' material substance. Despite the advances your civilization has made with ultrasound and related technologies, the concept of sound waves and their altering of matter tends to remain in some nebulous category of human mind, nesting somewhere at the outer borders of your credulity.

Perhaps more difficult still for you to imagine is that this simplistic example holds true for the entire Earth body, just as it does for any individual residing in the universe of matter. Anyone (the dark- or light-intended) determined to affect global alteration of a planet's energy body or any individual's energy field can aspire to just such a result...if only that magical measure, resonance, can be reached.

Consider the magnitude of such an hypothesis–that of the Earth (the macrocosm) or any human being (the microcosm) as a sort of cosmic wine glass, capable of being 'played' or shattered if the right vibrational formula is reached–and you may understand how very important it is that such technological and esoteric knowledge never end up in the hands of the ill-intentioned.

Unfortunately, the harnessing of the Gaian force (ownership of the planet's incalculable geophysical energy) was the intention of the alchemists of Atlán and it is again the ultimate desire of your modern day scientists–those assigned to serve the power elite. Their grasp far exceeds that of their predecessors, even thought the ancients' mastery of Earth's electromagnetic properties, the elemental energies and the power of the human mind was by far superior. We are telling you that the **intent** of the new breed is so absolutely focused that their command of the destructive powers that can be released upon you surpasses by light years the misguided efforts of the Dark Priesthood.

There lies the danger…for, as you well know, **it is the focused intent of any thought or action that determines the outcome.** Such is the foundation of all manifestation and that is where you, the lightworkers of Gaia, would be best advised to put your energies. In those landscapes–the fertile fields of your imagination–the mind's lens creates the physical world in which you still reside and your focus determines how you move about within it. United, the power of your focused thoughts and the love you bring forward through all actions, words and expression can deflect the polar forces of darkness and neutralize those intentions.

Bearing in mind what we have told you about the rise and fall of human civilizations, it should not surprise you that now, as you return to the apex point of your runaway technological prowess, you have reached the evolutionary threshold where you will, nonetheless, break it all down to start anew. Yet, this is different than before, when similar developments brought Atlantis to the sea bottom. At this evolutionary turn in planetary and human events, the Secret Government is only one step away from harnessing the energy of Gaia–a force inconceivable to you as individual units of the greater cosmic being. This time, they do truly have their fingers on the pulse of the Earth Mother and (we reiterate) they have the **focused intent** that is required to manifest just such an outcome.

Now, just a cosmic instant before your ascension out of the third dimension–your leap into the higher realms–they are determined to alter the planet's mental-emotional-physical body to a point that might very well interfere with her Process. They are dramatically close to succeeding…where in the past they have failed. This apex point marks like no other the clashing of extreme polar forces that is about to reach resolution in the next stage of Earth's evolution.

This phase is unlike any other in Gaia's millions of years of existence in the material universe because this is **ascension**. The planet has evolved to this point of spiritual progression and the dark forces know that their time of rule is running out.

Earth does move through the astral chords of your Solar Deity and into the fourth dimension. It is written in the Akasha, seen in the no-time. Yet, tampering with the vibrational body of Gaia can affect that process in ways that could create unimaginable destruction and suffering for all life forms upon the surface and within the inner world as well.

The clashing of the poles has never been greater than now, and you are all beginning to feel the acceleration. You are being pulled, pushed, numbed, activated, manipulated **and** assisted like never before. Remembering that there is nothing to fear will help you remain dauntless in the night of their darkness. Never forget that the greater your collective light, the lighter that darkness becomes. You, the loving beings of Gaia, have come to anchor the light that is required now and you are preparing for this on personal and planetary planes. We and others of the Galactic Federation have come to provide you with the information that has been held secret from you, so that you can operate in the light of knowledge and move forward.

Let us elaborate upon the controlling forces working to alter Earth's frequency and what their activities could mean on personal, planetary and galactic scales. Experiments similar to those that led to the demise of Atlantis are being executed now, in a military laboratory complex operating in the snow-covered lands of Alaska–home of the HAARP Project. The test areas of the experimental HAARP facility house an elaborate labyrinth of antennae, designed to transmit unimaginable levels of high-end radio frequencies into the ionospheric layer of Earth's etheric body–artificially heating the upper atmosphere–for reasons that are going to sound, at best, like science fiction to you. How could they not? What possible rational explanation could be found for disturbing Earth's natural energy fields...particularly at a time when the lower atmosphere–the ozone layer–has already reached the 'breaking point'? Yet, this is far from fiction, dear ones. This is reality in the very now of your physical lives. It is Dark Atlantis emerging.

Bear in mind that there are many layers of controls and misinformation operating in your world. The dark hierarchy currently presiding over Earth is stimulated by the Annunaki, antecedents of the power elite, or Secret Government. They, the invisible brokers of power of your Earth realm, are those who set the rules. It is they who place the players in the appropriate positions on the game board of your world–a landscape cut into imaginary boundaries (countries) that have been designed to look separate in order to make the game more intriguing and controllable.

The government leaders, who appear to you to guide and direct the military, economic and political strategies of your societies, are merely pawns in the game–and **they know it.** They understand enough of the structural nature of control to perform as they are told...to do what they have been assigned the seats of illusory power to do. In return for their obedience, they receive untold ego gratification, intense stimulation of the lower chakra energy centers and a place in contemporary written history.

Those who somehow dare to truly bring about change, forgetting that there is a power structure to which they must owe homage, are eventually eliminated. These are the assassinated peace leaders, the disarmed and disgraced who work for the freedom of humankind and the peaceful resolution of global conflicts and human suffering. Bold in their vision and determined of will, they are non-conformists who refuse to be 'team players' on the Power's game board. They call you to your own greatness, reminding you of what you are capable...and to what you are entitled. They stimulate all that is 'noble' within you, strengthening your awareness of how love, freedom and truth are your birthright. In essence, they encourage you to rebel against the dogma and hierarchy of control systems, exciting you to unity. They steer you away from the dark tunnels, always guiding you to the light.

Given what we have told you of the architects of power, it should be clear why the bright voices amongst you are labeled 'dangerous' and all-too-soon silenced. But do not despair over the loss of your heroes. Theirs is a karmic pact, which they accepted before coming into their respective incarnations. You must not feel tragedy or suffer their passing, for they are guiding you from other dimensions. They do leave their mark and inspiration for humankind, while continuing to work for you on other planes and those imprints are important…for they are your hope.

Do not fear that their message has been lost to you.

For many millennia of Earth time, countless lightworkers have had to operate in the shadows to avoid being persecuted by the Power—this is a reality charted throughout your written history and well beyond. But now, at this time of revolutionary brilliance throughout your solar system, more of you are stepping into the direct light of leadership, working for the good of the All. Nothing can stop you…unless you forget to embrace the other, letting go of all ego-centered consciousness, and spread the light from that place of unity and focused intent.

As to the hierarchy and their chain of command, we observe that select military officials and assigned scientists working under governmental proviso are often directly linked to the Secret Government, by-passing the figureheads of state. These key powers then transmit their orders to the second level. These are well-trained survival and power-centered individuals who truly believe in the need for weapons and surveillance against the ever-present 'enemy', those who believe in *Patria* and the 'only nation', unaware that there is only the One Governing Committee on Planet Earth.

Pro-HAARP propaganda coming from these Level Two military officials hails the project as a globally-relevant, scientific undertaking, intended to facilitate greater understanding of the Earth's atmosphere and global warming and at that level of protocol, they do sincerely believe it. Their understanding of the project is based upon very real concerns about ionospheric disturbance and its potential damaging effect upon global defense communications and surveillance satellites. That is their 'job'; they are trained to receive the briefings and to follow orders **without question.**

What is not being pronounced by the Level One military hierarchy is that one covert application of the HAARP Project is the creation of the ultimate weapon—one which will bring the entire planet to its knees. Once fully activated, HAARP will enable them to manipulate your world weather; control international communications and global surveillance; reconstruct the electromagnetic grid that once completely encircled Earth; and re-establish total dominance over the human personality (easily affected by changes in atmospheric pressure, lack of sunlight and altered electromagnetic frequencies).

Geophysical warfare—the harnessing of Earth's energies as a source of power—has the potential to alter the climate at determined points on the planet, cause changes in the ocean patterns, deflect and disrupt communications systems and stun entire populations. As diabolical as that sounds, is it any more shocking than the creation and deployment of the atomic bomb? Never forget that nuclear devastation was unleashed by the prophets of the New World Order such a short time ago that the elders amongst you actually still **hold the memory.**

Not surprisingly, the mass media rarely disturb that delicate area of your recall, for in that occasion (nuclear attack upon the so-called enemies of the 'free' world) the 'good' guys were the villains...and that is not the kind of realization the Power wishes to stimulate within your group consciousness. Compare the disproportionate ratio of anti-Hitler propaganda to the minimal recounting and depiction of the United States' vengeance upon the living beings of Hiroshima and Nagasaki and you will realize it is so. The truth is veiled as 'self-defense'—the misguided justification of all abuse of power—as fed to you by the architects of the perennial war being waged upon the innocent of Earth.

Still, not even the top military echelon are privy to the truth about HAARP–its enormity–nor would they be able to envision it...for, unlike the inner circle of the power elite, **they are not of Annunaki lineage.**

*          *          *

Just what is the ionosphere...and why should you, residents of Gaia, be concerned about what is being perpetrated out there, hundreds of miles above the surface?

The outer layer of Earth's field, which occupies a horizon located from about thirty-five to five hundred miles above the physical surface, is comprised of positively and negatively charged particles (known in your scientific terms as ions and protons), which are manifestations of your Sun's emanations throughout the extensive body of your solar system. It can be best described as plasma, a common energy form in the material universe, which serves as a shield against the infrared rays of your Solar Deity by regulating the amount of heat energy reaching your planet.

This plasmatic layer of Earth's being is of particular interest to commercial and military telecommunications, since it can reflect or absorb radio signals. It can amplify and distort them as well. This outer level of the interpenetrating layers of the atmosphere shield Earth from radiation, harmful frequencies and other deadly emanations from space. Yet, what we believe is its highest purpose for the life forms of Earth and especially for you, starseed of the Universe, is to filter the kind of deep space energy bombardment that can cause mutations in the DNA of all living beings on the Planet...letting pass into Earth's physical being only that which is appropriate for her evolution.

As ecologically concerned citizens of Planet Earth, you are well aware that industrial gases, automobile emissions and other waste products have seriously damaged the ozone layer. The holes or tears in this layer of Earth's protective energy shields are mapped for you (although you are still being denied the truth about the gravity of the situation). In these growing regions of ozone depletion, you are experiencing dangerous levels of ultraviolet light (UV and shorter, more damaging UVB waves) penetrating directly through to Earth, which is taking its toll on the biosphere and all living beings upon your world.

We see depletion of vast areas of phytoplankton in your oceans, those oxygen-producing life forms at the very bottom of your oceans' food chain. This is a little-publicized aspect of what should be one of your most urgent ecological concerns on Planet Earth and yet it is fundamental to the survival of your seas...as well as the skies above you. If Earth is to hold its atmosphere, balance between the sea, earth and sky must be re-established within your current decade. Your proliferation of carbon-burning fuels into the atmosphere and the poisoning of the oceans must be corrected **now.**

Ionospheric alteration is even more devastating than ultraviolet radiation, for this is the point of entry. This layer serves as the barrier that protects and nurtures the physical body of Gaia, an integral part of her equilibrium in every sense of the word. It is the destruction of the ionosphere (not the tearing apart of the ozone layer) that is your **greatest** peril. One tear there—one straw too many on the proverbial camel's back—will cause a biological and chemical chain reaction that will eradicate forever all but the subterranean civilizations of your species from the face of the Earth.

Like you, Gaia—the living deity—is a being of many dimensions, aspects and qualities manifesting at the physical, emotional, mental and astral levels. Her aura, the 'atmosphere', is (like yours) similarly composed of various 'layers', interpenetrating and interacting to perform much as the human aura does. In the case of Earth, your scientific community has studied and analyzed the aura, delineating certain layers (although there are no distinctly separate parts) as the ozone layer, the atmosphere, and the upper atmosphere, or the ionosphere. In humans, scientists are still reluctant to acknowledge these fields, while the aware amongst you understand that these aspects can be perceived as the mental, emotional and astral bodies–although in truth it is much more complex than that. Consciousness–the immensity of existence–defies finite descriptions and fixed terminology, but we are obliged to use them, so that we may elucidate our theories and relate to you in terms that are familiar to you.

The bodies of Gaia (her auric field) reach out hundreds of miles past her physical boundaries and it is at this level that the most significant changes are occurring. Just as your understanding of the human auric field has brought you to recognize that illness and disharmony originate in the auric body, so it is true for Earth, your Solar Deity and all other conscious entities that comprise the Universe. This is the basis of the physical reality. It is necessary that you understand this principal law of existence before we can adequately describe to you the nature of Earth resonance, and how disharmony in her auric field (from the lower layers of the atmosphere to the outer limits–the ionosphere) can result in total upheaval upon and within Earth's physical body.

Therefore, building upon what we have told you of electromagnetic frequencies and resonant waves, we ask you to imagine one weapon powerful enough to entrain the entire global civilization–the planet itself–and you will understand why bombs and military arsenals are as antiquated to the military as ink wells and quills are to the modern day writers of your computer generation.

Imagine what could be achieved if the scientific/military community were to reach resonance with the entire planet...to use Earth, in a metaphorical sense, to shatter glass! We are suggesting here that what is brewing in Alaska is just such a scheme–the idea of blasting the auric field of Earth, the ionosphere, with enough gigawatts of high-end radio frequency to alter her etheric being: her mental, emotional and physical bodies! You, the creatures of Earth, will so be altered as well, for you are the reflection of the Goddess and are subject to the laws that govern her being.

In *The Cosmos of Soul*, we asked you to consider the potential here: *"What if the vibrational pace-setter were of the dark intention? Suppose one or more individuals, who would control others for personal or political gain, were intent upon imposing some form of mental stimulation that would set up another form of entrainment: a pre-determined frequency intended to create certain desired chemical changes to occur within the receiver?"*

Those assigned military leaders, the Level One puppets of the power elite, believe they are working on the perfect weapon, designed to harness the enormous power of Gaia against the elusive 'enemy', just as it is intended to keep the populace under control. And this is true, at that level, for there are many layers of operation and intent involved here. They are perfecting the weapon of weapons and they are correct in believing that their covert and subliminal controls over you will be vastly intensified, but this is nothing compared to what will result from the tampering of the shield—the ionospheric layer of Gaia's auric field.

**Listen carefully.**

All the weapons of destruction currently known to exist throughout your world—the nuclear arsenals; chemical and biological warfare; sophisticated air and space-going craft and 'intelligent' missiles—are going to be totally obsolete when HAARP is fully operative. You do not want to know what will be unleashed at full power. The build-up of these electromagnetic emissions, the frequency that reaches resonance with Gaia's *wam*, is the trigger that will shatter the rhetorical glass. It will, indeed, cause unfathomable upheaval within and above the Earth, just as it will disturb all life on your surface world. Moreover, we reiterate: it could very well interfere with your ascension—your passage through the vortex—as we have described it to you in our earlier transmissions.

Enough of you have begun to research and divulge your information to the seekers of truth to know what is in store for you if HAARP is allowed to continue. Most others have not even heard of HAARP until now, for there, in the Alaskan icelands, it is remote enough to evade your full-scale investigation and **that is deliberate.**

Global awareness of the project—the probing of a concerned population—would upset the progress of the experiments currently being perpetrated on the atmosphere and in the underground. But you must know about HAARP if you are to understand how the Secret Government intends to manipulate Gaian energy at its most forceful, just as their ancestors attempted in the Last Generation. You must know just what is being unleashed from the snowy white fields of that relatively unknown laboratory. You must know, children of the stars, what dangerous designs are once again being drawn for Planet Earth, as they were then...in the days of Dark Atlantis.

There, in the remote lands of the chilling Alaskan tundra, military scientists are developing the awesome capacity to blast the ionospheric layer of your planet's atmosphere with what can be measured (in your terminology) as one hundred billion watts of high-end radio frequencies. Unbeknownst to most of the human population, their experiments are already operating at 8-10% of that colossal force. They have been actively building up the charge being beamed into the ionosphere and are already working with over eight billion watts of high-end radio frequencies.

The Project has, as its primary objective, the deliberate heating of the ionosphere (much like microwave heats your food). It is intended to stimulate the ionic particles in the upper atmosphere, in an attempt to manipulate certain electromagnetic reactions–reactions that are of particular interest to the Power and believed by the Annunaki to be of absolute necessity to the future of Nebiru.

You have been shown the beginnings of HAARP's effect upon your world in these years. We refer particularly to the Earth calendar of 1997-1998, when HAARP output was turned up substantially, abnormally raising the ionospheric temperature. Gaia responded with a violence that ripped across the surface as hurricanes, floods, tornadoes, drought and pestilence. The 'free' scientific community, uninformed of the covert developments in Alaska, explained this unprecedented catastrophe as the 'El Niño Effect', which the human population en large accepted as a natural phenomenon.

It is true...that which your scientific community has identified as the El Niño Effect has long existed as a geophysical phenomenon on Earth;

we do not wish to infer that it is not so. Rather, it is our observation that its force and, subsequently, its manifestations have been exacerbated by human disturbance of Earth's auric body: global warming; toxic emissions; chemical and bacterial spraying; negative thoughts of collective human consciousness; the growing force of HAARP bombardment of Earth's upper atmosphere.

There are other signs...strange incidents that can no longer be explained away as 'natural'. You have begun to experience lightning bolts appearing from cloudless skies—the cause of frightening and 'unexplainable' electrical outages and reactions about you. You have heard that as if from nowhere, large fragments of ice are simply falling from thin air, crashing down upon your city streets with an eerie vengeance.

Others, the more sensitive amongst you, are feeling disturbingly 'electrified', as if some subtle current were running from your crowns down into your soles and (in select areas of North America) that is exactly what is happening. This is one of the intended capabilities of the HAARP Project, whose emanations over specific geographical areas can interfere with and deflect the kundalini energy rising from your lower chakras up the byways of your natural meridians: the Ida and Pingala energy channels. It is a way to keep you blocked in the lower chakras...and isn't that the intention of those who would own you?

To the HAARP scientists—the top-level administrators—you are laboratory animals and your cages (the manipulated electromagnetic force fields of Gaia) are far more interesting than the individual human beings and other life forms that will suffer from their effects. Therefore, prepare yourselves...for these are only the beginnings of odd disturbances and suffering which will soon become commonplace in your current experience, as the pressure cooker is turned up on Earth's upper atmosphere. Only the beginnings...

We ask that you consider very carefully what we are about to tell you before reacting to it—from a place of centeredness and calm. We wish to provide the provocation that will help you formulate the questions; to pay closer attention; to challenge and to speak out. We wish not to upset but to stimulate you, for your heightened awareness of what goes on around you is now of the utmost importance. This is required of you if you are truly to affect change in your world and to participate as conscious beings in the dynamic evolution of your society, your world, and the galaxy.

Most importantly, it is your **liberation**.

*        *        *

From our vantage point, we observe the real purpose of HAARP as immensely greater than what we have described to you thus far, and this we intend to share with you by elaborating the ramifications of this deadly technology for you...citizens of Planet Earth.

We reiterate that the Secret Government is determined, at this time of revolutionary change in the consciousness of Gaia, to identify the vibrational quantum that can play Earth, the being, like the chalice until it begins its musical emissions–that electromagnetic vibration that signals its wam or soul note. As fantastic as it sounds, they are, indeed, seeking to reach resonance with Gaia and utilize the enormous, unfathomable energies that would be released with such power for much more than global domination and mere tampering with the human spirit.

We suggest that what is behind the project, the intention of the Power, is to control that enormous geophysical force by means of technological domination of the planet's electromagnetic frequencies, controlling all life forms as well–absolute dominion over Planet Earth. They believe that once they have determined the electromagnetic heartbeat, the thought wave oscillations and the soul song of Planet Earth, they will actually be able to establish resonance between Earth and Nebiru–a cosmic connection so intense that the two beings will be inexorably linked through the no-time of their existence.

Why? It is their deviate plan to create such a powerful vibratory linkage that Earth will draw Nebiru back from its galactic course through cold space and through the astral tunnels of your Solar Deity, as the entire system ascends. And they are dangerously on track, for this is not as impossible as it sounds to you, surface dwellers of a planetary body in material space. To those who have surpassed the experience of individuality (the illusion of separateness), the concept of individual celestial bodies is also extremely limited. In the All-That-Is, there is no true separation, for all is vibrationally linked and interrelated. Therefore, although talk of planetary link-up surely may border on the ridiculous to most, we confirm that it is absolutely possible to think in these terms and to aspire to such cosmic grandeur.

Your race, directed by the Annunaki, has reached this phase of development. We remind you that finding a stellar home has been the objective of the Nebiruans from that remote time in celestial shifting when they were flung out of Sirius. It should not surprise you that they are pulling out all the stops now, at the time of your Solar Deity's ascension into the fourth dimension. It is now or never.

In Late Atlantis, the Annunaki lords attempted just such a form of energy linkage between the two planets, for they had orchestrated this symphony long ago. It was this aspect of experimentation with the primordial forces of Earth that caused the sinking of an entire continent, of tidal waves and flooding over most of your world—the dark night of sunless winter for a vast time on the face of the Earth. Had the Atlanteans been working with the type of devices being utilized in the HAARP facility, the results might very well have been much, much different.

$$*\qquad\qquad*\qquad\qquad*$$

What if this unfathomable scenario were to actually be achieved: planetary link-up between Gaia and Nebiru? What would this mean to Earth residents: the humans, animals and plant beings?

It is essential that you understand karmic process. Nebiru, the wanderer, has chosen to evolve much more slowly than the planetary beings of your Solar Deity. That planet cannot achieve ascension simply by surfing Earth's wave length, for that, in the end, is what we are talking about here. We all come in to 'do the work'; not even the great celestial beings are an exception to the Divine Plan. There are no short cuts in our return to All-That-Is. This is the way and the glory of Spirit.

Nonetheless, HAARP best be disarmed before the scientists, in the bungling of their experiments (their mindless abuse of Earth energies), cause any further disruption to the auric body of your planet. As your Solar Deity prepares for emergence, storms, solar flares and explosions are being processed at the ionospheric level of Gaia's outer being and these events are essential aspects of her conversion, as they are yours. They are the vital manifestations of matter as it experiences transmutation—reflections of the conscious deity—and there must be no interference from the wanton technicians of control.

**Your rebellion can bring down the transmitters**...but it must be through peaceful resistance, or the Power will find the excuse it needs to destroy you. Your collective mind—the focused consciousness of the many—can deflect the bombarding energy and heal disharmony on any level. Your strength is in your clarity, unity and intent. Seek to reveal that which is hidden and speak that truth to all those who can hear.

Through the electronic static and hum of their controlling devices, the Goddess strains to hear the pulse of the One Heart—the voice of your souls. You must move more quickly than ever before, for it is one minute to midnight and all is not peaceful on Planet Earth.

# Chapter 9

## Tesla,
## Alchemist of Atlán

Those of you who know about free energy technology–the progress and suppression of it–no doubt have been anticipating our mention of Nikola Tesla somewhere earlier in these transmissions. Others may have yet to hear of the man whose revolutionary contributions in the field of physical science laid much of the groundwork for the 21st century technologies to which we have alluded. He has been greatly ignored in the historical record, excluded from the mainstream myths and misinformation that surround your scientific and technological advancements. And yet, the former Atlantean alchemist has left his imprint in ways that are only now being recognized for the impact it has had upon your world.

At this time of absolute technological and industrial frenzy, it is only natural that the ecologists amongst you seek the alternative methodologies that have helped create a cult hero of Nikola Tesla. Indeed, his original intention to bring free energy to the peoples of Gaia was a humanitarian mission of the highest intentions, and you do long for heroes in a world of dark warriors.

As you exhume from the public record the list of his inventions, you can only be amazed at the accomplishments of a man who so clearly pioneered much of your modern applications of electromagnetism, while educating contemporary and future scientists to the potential power available on planetary and cosmic planes. Had he not been sabotaged by the corporate giants (agents of the Secret Government) who monopolize the energy supplies of your planet, you could very well have been spared the ecological crises resulting from their exploitation of Earth's rich resources. Moreover, had he not been manipulated by those same power players, Tesla may never have swung back over to the dark side of his own genius. That, again, is karma playing itself out as one of many probable realities which the soul creates on many levels...in and beyond the physical realm.

Nonetheless, at a time when you are destroying the atmosphere, oceans and soil with the waste of carbon fuels and leaking radiation at all points of the planet, Tesla's commitment to providing free, clean energy can easily be construed as a noble quest. Be circumspect, however, in your evaluation of this individual, for the pressures of that lifetime, his unresolved ego consciousness and those karmic patterns sabotaged his primary intent. We wish to suggest that if you pore more deeply into the works of Nikola Tesla, you may recognize that his inventions were far more destructive than you currently understand them to be. Further, we propose that the effects of his experiments have everything to do with the dilemma that you are all now facing on Planet Earth.

At the time of his entry into that physical form (mid-nineteenth century), your scientific and technical prowess were still in the infancy stage. Yet, you were progressing at a rapid pace, where science and spirit were struggling to hold the balance and the pendulum swung back and forth, setting the rhythm of human evolution. Tesla was to catapult you into other frameworks of consciousness, disturbing that equilibrium, for his imprint was from the 'future' and the 'past'...from the no-time of all experience.

This was no ordinary mortal. The one, Nikola Tesla, journeyed from a galaxy far beyond your current understanding of 'distance' and 'time', to take human form for the first time during the era of the Last Generation of Atlantis. We are telling you that the man, Tesla, walked amongst the native Atlanteans during the Last Generation, but that his was an **alien presence**. We further affirm that his assimilation into that culture was, in large part, coordinated by the Annunaki for purposes not unlike those elaborated in the previous transmission. He never underwent the tedium of incarnation. He simply walked into the body of a priest of the Dark Brotherhood—one who happily handed over his physical being, eager to release from his misguided loyalties and the dark persuasion.

He, *Akkaeneset—Keeper of the Energy,* was assigned by the Annunaki ruling elite the supreme position of Chief Alchemist of Atlán. There, the time traveler found a technologically sophisticated people, whose abilities with crystal technology had reached a significant phase of development. He observed the Atlanteans' mastery of 'mind over matter', and their ability to focus and direct human brain waves to create the energy needed to illuminate the cities and to power much of their technology. Although by his standards rudimentary, the mindlight generators were structures of a visionary society, which he knew would embrace much more sophisticated applications of its own inventions. In so doing, he would further steer the Dark Priesthood down its path of domination over the populace, fueling Annunaki desire for the control and subjugation of the entire human race.

Before the Dark Priesthood began its mind manipulation campaign against the people, the mindlight generator network was pure light; it was the quintessential model of the interface of human intelligence with the elemental forces of the planet, united for the higher purpose of humankind's advancement. To fully understand its significance, it is important that you be able to conceptualize how the people energized the crystals networks by focusing their intent to transmute stored consciousness into physical energy.

Although still perceived by many as 'magic', the manifestation of thought as physical expression is so commonplace in your reality that most of the time you simply overlook it. Then, there is the question of focus, for most of modern human culture is distracted and your energies are often scattered. Yet, surely you have known that wondrous moment when you are so clearly determined upon an outcome that nothing blurs your vision and you find almost instantly that it manifests before your eyes. You may best recognize your abilities in simple actions, when your need or desire is so great that you can focus only on a specific result, such as creating a place for your automobile when you simply must park, or a last-minute cancellation at an event that you absolutely must attend. Imagine an entire population, disciplined in the focused use of their minds and aware of the power of their thoughts, uniting to realize a common goal!

The Last Generation Atlanteans found their strength as a civilized people in their superb ability to bring to manifestation one supreme desire: that the All be served with the boundless energies of the Earth Mother and the collective mind. The heart centers of the population were wide open during those morning hours of ritual and their devotion to the well-being of the entire community was unconditional. No doubt you are developing a much deeper awareness of the power of thought over matter now, as you begin the shift out of material reality. Surely it is becoming easier for you to envision the awesome creative force of the One Mind and the potential of your unification.

We assure you that the Atlanteans' ability to energize the crystal generators with the power of their focused intent was as natural to them as 'flipping the switch' is to you. Every home and work environment housed a central worship crystal; all temple complexes centered around a great spheroid quartz; all gathering places and rest areas provided crystal meditation areas. Whole cities depended upon this constancy of thought and concentration; their free energy was formed of it. It was a prototype civilization of cooperation, respect for the forces of nature, and devotion to the celestial deities—those of the family of Ra (your solar system) and many beyond.

You can imagine why the Dark Side found a fertile field in which to seed and then harvest the fear and negative energies that would eventually dominate the once golden lands of ancestral humanity. The people of

Atlantis were innocent, yet capable of great focus of intent and they knew, on many levels, how to harness earth energies. They were perfect fodder for the preying beast...food for the hungry of Nebiru.

Returning to the mindlight generators, we ask that you contemplate the power of the collective consciousness–focused, as it was at that time, on the specific purpose of serving the All. Consider the immensity of that immeasurable electromagnetic frequency of mind, united with the primordial forces of Gaia. Can you envision how this profound human effort could be channeled into the crystals, drawing electrical charges through the orichalcum coils of the generators, to light and energize the energy channels above ground?

Aren't you reliving this in mutated form? Consider your worship of the 'almighty' computers, which literally run your world. They, too, are based upon silicates and, although you are less aware of your direct involvement with them, you do empower and energize your computers through the collective consciousness. Let us say that the Atlanteans did so consciously, while yours is a process operating at the subconscious level of group mind–a level that is being imprinted by the architects of control. By giving your power to the computer, you are giving it to the designers of mass consciousness. You are handing your intelligence over to them as well; your bodies–even your souls–are imprinted.

Moreover, you are turning your planetary home over to the mechanical masters and you have begun to see the results of that abandon all around you. The video syndrome of 21st century humanity is disempowering you completely and, as in Atlantis, the dark ones have infiltrated your collective and are entraining you and the children via that medium.

Contemporary technology, like the mindlight generator networks, is a most effective management tool. Yet, there is a striking difference. Whereas computers and televisions are constructed of artificial realities that create in the mass consciousness a form of entrainment far more dangerous than that of Atlantis, the mindlight generators were the **vehicles** of the collective mind. That is, before the interference began, the generators served the highest purpose: the good of the All. This has never been the case of modern technology, which has almost always been the vehicle of the Power and used against you. It is important that you make this distinction, for most of you worship technology and cannot accept its destructive implications, nor have you understood how it is de-humanizing you.

They are on the verge of turning your world over to robotic rule…this is the next phase. Imagine a world run by artificial intelligence, as it has already begun to manifest, and you will realize that such creations would be your demise. The greatness of being human would be lost forever, for all that is beautiful and just about you would be usurped by the mechanical gods of your own assembly.

We, who look upon you as great fountains of love and intense emotion—the dreamers of the Universe—cannot imagine how you can give your humanness over so willingly, and yet we understand how you are manipulated to do just that. It is a reflection of that which you are told is the 'natural' progression of your species, however unnatural it truly may be.

Remember that the inevitable quest of science is to exceed all previous achievements; it is the nature of intelligence to build upon that which it has already acquired. This translates in common experience as a feeling that "if we can do this, then we can surely do this other". Learning is a building process of acquisition that all intelligent beings eventually experience, more so in societal structures, where you interact and build upon each other's progressive knowledge. Whether that process swings dark or light is largely determined by the levels of consciousness that are being expressed in one's environment during his or her time of passing in body—the time the soul spends in 'school'. Let us not forget that there are influences from outside or beyond the physical reality, for there are myriad aspects of interpenetrating consciousness (direct and indirect intervention), which can affect probable outcomes.

Akkaeneset was fascinated by the far-reaching possibilities of acquired Atlantean know-how, while the Dark Priesthood was predominantly interested in establishing control over the society. A former master of the physical laws of the material universe, he experimented with low-range frequency emissions, which were beamed into the coils and crystals of the underground energy system. His intention was to study and record the effect that different frequencies would have upon the populace. He was determined to identify the range of emissions that would most effectively stimulate the population to higher levels of generation and amplification of geophysical reactions from the Earth...there, in the subterranean chambers that lined the cities.

The setting of these mind-altering emissions at pre-established frequencies could evoke depression or despair in the people, and this could be observed as a widespread phenomenon. In those instances, the mindlight generators no longer produced enough energy to light the cities. Other ranges of electromagnetic pulse could provoke rage and sexual passion, responses that would cause huge surges of energy to race up the coils and overload the Atlantean circuitry. This was entertaining to the Alchemist, who had never encountered anything quite like the body of human emotions and he marveled at how its deliberate manipulation could affect the energy flow of the greater planetary being.

As Akkaeneset's work progressed, the Dark Priesthood gained a stronghold over the society, intensifying the entrainment of the Atlanteans during rituals of prayer and devotion. We believe that there is no greater abuse of power than the bold and deliberate sabotage of any sovereign individual's spiritual experience; there can be no darker intention. In those moments, when you open your crowns to bathe in the light of Prime Creator, you are as birds in flight–soaring beyond limitation, knowing your godliness. To interfere in that connection to Divinity can only be construed as total and deliberate intervention in the spiritual awakening of a sovereign being...and that is against all the principles of Creation.

Through the developments achieved in Akkaeneset's underground laboratories, the cloaked ones broke the electromagnetic code of human emotionality–a series of frequencies that could evoke desired emotional reactions, control and even destroy the human mind. They developed the methodology that would subliminally chain people to the lower chakra emotions of fear, rage and sexuality for the express purpose of heightening the energy fields of their technology and intensifying their power. Meanwhile, Akkaeneset was increasingly mesmerized by Earth's interaction with human mind and emotion, becoming almost obsessive in his desire to push human emotion and the forces of Gaia to the breaking point.

Bear in mind that, even then, the Annunaki of Earth were designing planetary link-up with Nebiru. They believed Akkaeneset capable of the kind of breakthroughs that would finally show them the way to establish resonance with Earth and draw Nebiru into Ra's system forever. He was given total power to realize that objective, enjoying absolute freedom, wealth and pleasure. And, of course, he was totally free to manipulate the people of Atlantis and to use their established technology **as well as their spirit** to affect the ultimate goal of reeling Nebiru into a permanent orbit along with you.

Thus, experimentation with the geophysical forces of Earth took place well before your modern times...well before the Power began its destructive assembly of antennae in the Alaskan fields. The one, Akkaeneset, turned the Earth inside out, pulling and pushing, creating technologies that far surpass those you know or imagine today. He performed important experiments with gravity, invisibility, electricity; he and his team gave the Priesthood the power to fly craft at great distances; there were solar ships, time machines and laser rays far more sophisticated than yours. The most significant aspect of his walking amongst your ancestors, however, was yet another.

A time traveler, to the 3D framework the Alchemist brought acquired knowledge so far ahead of Earth time that he actually tore a hole in the linear time construct of that reality. He pulled humankind, in a sense, out of time-in-a-line and showed your race glimpses of fourth dimensional reality. Ironically, while providing the Priesthood the means of entraining the minds of your ancestors, he simultaneously gave to humanity the vision of that which lies beyond the constraints of the third dimension. This was the dual nature of his being amongst you; it was his greatest contribution to humankind.

Speaking repeatedly as we do of the no-time, consider that if you are currently moving toward technologies that already existed 13,000 years ago, in the underground laboratories and power plants of Atlán, then you are moving forward and backward at the same time. This concept may seem foreign to you now, but it will become much clearer to you in the near future. You are tearing through many barriers now; time is warping and rips in three-dimensional reality are beginning to occur with some constancy as you begin the process of ascension.

Akkaeneset's reappearance in physical reality was determinedly a soul quest to resolve his Atlantean lifetime of dark intent, for his karmic debt was immense. As Chief Alchemist of Atlán, he was not only directly involved in the experiments that brought the destruction of that reality. He was the mastermind of the Atlantis Error—its creator—and this he remembered. His tampering with the geophysical forces of Earth and the disruption of human emotional fields simply blew a fuse in the neural networks of Gaia. The sinking of Atlantis and the ensuing global devastation was simply that: Planet Earth was short-circuited and her central nervous system was shut down and lain to rest. Gaia, in essence, reclaimed her power.

After the devastation of that lifetime, the soul of Akkaeneset chose not to return to form until that time when he would be provided the opportunity to right the scales and his karmic debt could be released of the burden of the Error. The 'time' was 1856—a turning point for humanity—the beginning of the Industrial Age. Nikola Tesla passed from the womb of the mother, through the portal and was born, bringing into the incarnation his innate knowledge of the workings of the Cosmos and a not-so-remote memory of his Atlantean misdoings.

As a young man, he dedicated almost all of his energies to the study of the exchange and interaction of electricity and magnetism, and how these forces can be directed and harnessed with the power of the mind. Is it any wonder? Dedicated, as he was, to exposing humanity to the awesome power of these contrasting and complimentary forces, he returned to form to teach you the ancient lesson–to show you how to utilize the forces of Gaia to serve the light, rather than to amplify the darkness. This was his karmic purpose.

As you are well aware, resolution of karma often involves confronting the same temptations and tests of previous lifetimes, and these are often much greater and far more difficult to overcome. In the case of Akkaeneset, the good intentions of a soul-healing-karma eventually lost to the pressures of Earth life and the unbearable burden of super-human genius.

We confirm that his early years as Nikola Tesla were, indeed, dedicated to bringing free energy to the entire planet, in order to serve humankind at another of its many junctures on the highway of ascension. As a student of physics, he also dreamt of affecting changes in the weather, to serve those who suffered from drought, unbearable heat and cold and other unlivable climates. A young inventor, he envisioned global communications, bringing the peoples of your world closer, and even imagined traveling through time–to the future and to the past–for the expansion of humankind's experience in the 3D theater. Most significantly, he dreamed of harnessing Earth's geophysical forces, for reasons that lay in the cool, dark waters of his subconscious.

Like the Adept Einstein, Tesla was dedicated to gifting humanity with a technology that could corral the forces of Nature for the good of humankind...ending all famine, all suffering in the world. His initial intention was to bring the light of universal wisdom to the expanse of humanity's physical world and to empower the race with what he believed would be utilized for the good of all societies upon your planet. His noble idea was to utilize the natural forces of Gaia to bring free energy to the beings of Earth.

Unfortunately, that was not the master plan of the power elite, whose marketing strategy for Planet Earth has always been formulated on a much less altruistic foundation. Stripping the planet for profit and forcing the race into consumption of those stolen resources for its survival have been the design imposed upon humankind from the onset of Annunaki controls over humanity, so many thousands of years before your written record.

Although his early intentions were those of high purpose, the man, Nikola Tesla, unfortunately still had unresolved ego issues that were easily played by the Power, for this is their meat: the unresolved ego. Tesla knew that harnessing the power of such physiological forces would change Earth's global reality forever. Unfortunately, his extra-dimensional vision of Gaia's geophysical potential as a source of free energy for all human beings was rejected by the corporate owners of Earth's resources, for they were already selling you energy. They mounted a fierce campaign against him, until the ridicule and discrediting of his ideas were so insurmountable that his claims of free energy for all of humanity became the joke of the scientific world.

Disenchanted, Tesla began to turn his genius back to the dark side. He was soon called upon by the sentinels of the power elite, the military leaders, who set about monopolizing his work through extensive financial grants and access to the kind of equipment that only they could provide. This, of course, was part of the scheme to simply remove him from the public arena, where he might get enough attention to upset the plans of the Secret Government. He was set up in a controlled laboratory environment, where he was free to design and develop his innovative energy machines for the United States military and 'sympathetic' private enterprise.

So it was that his energies were redirected and his intention sabotaged, for the Power never intended to gift humankind with such a liberating resource. Nikola Tesla succumbed to his need for recognition, turning his knowledge over to the dark forces of the military. His earlier visions of free energy for all humanity and liberation from linear time were eventually replaced with designs of controlling Atlantean devices, memories he brought through to be confronted once again as karmic choice.

During this period, he reported having perfected a 'death beam' of such intensity that it could pull thousands of aircraft from the skies, just as it could drop entire battalions of enemy soldiers dead in their tracks. He was, indeed, speaking of that very technology that caused the island to sink into the ocean floor, shaking Earth right down to its core and destabilizing the auric field through to the outer layers of the atmosphere.

Tesla activated his 'Death Ray' apparatus at the turn of the century. It resulted in an explosion in the remote lands of Siberia that was so vast and destructive that not even an atomic blast could have exceeded its impact. This historic event has been explained away as the crash of a meteor or a comet impacting Earth, but the devastation that remained in the fields of Tunguska were actually the manifestation of the alchemist's mad invention.

The soul of the one incarnating as Nikola Tesla had once again chosen power over love; it chose the individual ego over the One Heart…and that choice changed forever the destiny of Planet Earth. As in Atlantis, the knowledge of such power was to shape the existence of all beings on the planet…indeed, of the very planet itself.

In support of our analysis of HAARP and its real purpose, we remind you that Tesla was quoted in his later years as predicting that "one day energy would be transmitted to another planet". What was not spoken in that declaration was his subconscious memory of the Annunaki plan to improve upon his 'resonance detonator' and use it to reel in Nebiru, just as the new architects of the Atlantean 'Death Ray'–the HAARP technicians–are attempting to do from the Alaskan fields.

Do you suppose he walks once more, there–in the soiled snows of Armageddon?

# Chapter 10

## Ra

In the midst of all their tampering with the celestial deities and human beings, the geophysical forces of Earth and the very music of creation, Ra's transmutational revolution has been creating all kinds of unwelcome and unforeseen disturbance in the immediate activities and future plans of the Power—plans that revolve around your Sun's ascension process, Earth's passing from material reality and the destiny awaiting Nebiru.

There is so much your species does not know about the Sun and that is a paradox, considering its definitive role in the cosmic events that have led to the blossoming of life upon the Earth—the very birthing of the planet! Were you to examine the remaining written records of ancient astronomers and the astrologers of old, you most surely would come away with a feeling that your ancestors were far more intrigued with the nature of the Sun than they were the planets of your solar system, the Moon or the distant stars of the night skies. It is as if, with your expanding aware-ness of the heavenly bodies, your zealous discoveries of new planets, their moons and the asteroid belt have distracted your attention away from the Center of your celestial home—**until now.**

It appears to those who observe you from a 'distance' that you seem to take the Sun for granted, or that you are distracted with more 'earthly' cares, or that perhaps it has been just too complex to contemplate and too remote to warrant much of your attention.

Contemporary Earth society, as a whole, has severed the ancients' emotional connection with your Solar Deity, forsaking what was once an intuitive appreciation of its divinity. Only the indigenous peoples, those who
hold the records, still worship the Sun in that way. Therefore, we shall
assume it safe to say that you are much less appreciative of the Sun than
the late Atlanteans, whose entire culture was formed around their worship
of the Light Bearer, Ra–your celestial 'father'.

Indeed, religious indoctrination over the last millennium taught you that
the celebration of the heavenly bodies as 'divine beings' were pagan rites and
witchery. You were burned for such beliefs–beaten into submission.
Meanwhile, the great books of astrological wisdom and celestial magic either
went up in flames or were buried in the private libraries of the religious
authority, as if knowledge were theirs to suppress and deny you.

Nonetheless, it is important that you recognize Ra as the key to your
ascension, for it is the Sun that initiates the passage through its astral
chords and it is the Sun that pulls you into the next dimension. The body
of the Deity (the planets, moons and celestial bits and pieces that hold
orbit along with you) moves through as an aspect of solar ascension–just
as you, the awakening of Gaia, ascend as an aspect of her procession out of
the material universe and into the fourth dimension. Therefore, know that
you are being absolutely guided through this process, as Ra actively prepares your entire cosmic family for passage through the astral chords of his
transmutation onto yet higher planes of consciousness.

Earth and her sister planets are to the Sun as you are to Gaia–consciousness units of the greater being. All is in cosmometric proportion and
every piece of the multidimensional puzzle fits perfectly into the other,
swirling into the supreme vortex that is drawing you from the density of
the material realm into the higher dimensions.

**You can see how yours is a very small part of a very big galactic event.**

The Sun has entered its most intense phase of transformation now, as
have Earth, her sister deities, you, the animals, plants and rocks of Gaia.
At the time of this transmission, it is accelerating with a rapidity that will

soon exceed anything your scientists can monitor or record in logical and technical terminology. Ra is undergoing enormous shifts in his energy fields, throwing off more and more of his material body (the particles and bits of its atomic essence). He is exploding in great solar flares, blasting increased levels of solar radiation out to the far reaches of the solar system and beyond, into outer space.

This is metamorphosis, the throwing off of quantum sums of stored energy in preparation for the imminent experience of passage and transmutation of form. This stage of that process is manifesting as extraordinary solar phenomena. They are being observed by distant civilizations and studied by the government teams, the 'free' scientists and amateur astronomers amongst you, who (like us) are focused upon the shifting fabric of your galaxy.

More of you are tuning in to the experience of Ra's emergence on psychic levels, for you are being beamed the cosmic waves that facilitate that aspect of your evolutionary progression. There are many degrees of psychic attunement and different times in which you 'blossom', which is why some of you are leaping boldly forward, while others are still stepping ever-so-lightly off the tried and true paths of analytical thought and into the space of inner knowing.

For those who have yet to develop the intuitive faculty, there are more than enough graphic images and data available outside of the secret laboratories to provide them with convincing evidence of what is actually taking place on celestial scales. Thanks to your space agency's 1995 launch of SOHO (Solar and Heliospheric Observatory Spacecraft) and the proliferation of sophisticated mass telescope facilities in various key locations around the world, images of solar flares, magnetic storms, sunspots, whirling energy vortices and ejecting plasma are now being made available to the public. They are bringing the picture of the Sun's temperament and its manifestations into the eye of human scrutiny, while the technicians of the Power are recording your Solar Deity's vibrational codes.

Enough of the free scientists now have access to instruments which monitor cosmic events (however limited the capacity of such technology) that the government teams are being forced to reveal some of their classified data regarding the Sun's 'erratic' behavior to the rest of the world. Elaborate studies are being conducted of these heightened solar flares, increasingly intense solar radiation and many other 'top priority' concerns having to do with the shifting energies of Ra and their effect on Earth and the rest of the solar system. Let us say that members of the scientific community–those working to expand your horizons as well as those seeking to limit them –are watching with awe and concern the eruptive chain of solar events that they expect will crest in 2001.

You may be aware that solar activity has been identified as reaching a peak in its cycle every eleven Earth years. This fits like a precision watch with the Mayan calendar, for it is eleven years later (at the completion of the year 2012) that the Fifth Sun, the closing of time, occurs in the Mayan record. It was witnessed through the crystal skulls…observed in the no-time.

Let us assure you that what is being observed as 'intense solar activity' now is but a fizzle compared to what is going to occur at the closing of your calendar year 2012. That, curious ones, marks the beginning of a solar extravaganza the likes of which not even the Nebiruans (distant viewers of Sirian ascension) can claim ancestral memory.

This is, nonetheless, an unprecedented time of solar 'disturbance'. You now are witness to these outbursts as they are occurring in a sort of 'real time' perspective, thanks to enhanced computer imaging capabilities. Accurate images of the continuous explosions and pyrotechnics of this hyperactive phase of solar activity are readily available to you now. This is one very positive aspect of your technology.

Like some magnificent fireworks exhibition, huge tongues of plasma shoot out from the Sun and then, following the magnetic field lines of its massive form, turn back into its nuclear body to form great loops of gaseous, plasmatic fire. Solar flares throw off enormous levels of radiation;

sunspots appear with much more frequency; the solar wind that moves through the solar system blows with far greater intensity than ever before.

Something really unusual must be going on out there, wouldn't you agree?

*         *         *

The power elite observe and study these celestial fires with due consternation. As Ra erupts in violent solar storms, unparalleled in their intensity and frequency, the Secret Government cautiously monitors their effects in 'earthly' terms. They are nervously watching and waiting to see what all this solar exuberance is going to mean to their covert space programs; to the proliferation of satellites in Earth's orbit and beyond; to their surveillance and communications systems and, lest we forget, to the **HAARP Project**.

We observe your satellite clutter, penetrating ever deeper into sacred space as it attempts to provide the 'privileged' not only the images but also the vibrational data to analyze and explore what lies beyond and ahead of you. Of the full-scale probing of solar combustion and its interaction with the ionosphere, there is far more activity than you can imagine, for they are totally focused upon the Sun's dynamics and the interference this disturbance is causing to their Survival Plan.

To this end, the Power prefers to limit your awareness of the Sun's fluctuations and their effect upon human nature and the global environment. They would prefer to deny you (the financiers of their experiments) any access whatsoever to their spatial impressions and chemical analyses of the atmosphere, for they are busy there…operating in near secrecy. Consider the effect uncontrollable solar disruption can have upon the weakening grid, global communications systems, their covert technologies and, most importantly, human behavior…and you may understand why the Secret Government has become so much more Atlantean in its preoccupation with the behavior of your Solar Deity and ever so much more evasive about its findings.

Know that Ra has the teams scrambling for solutions. These fierce solar flares, unlike anything ever recorded in your written record, are intensifying at a time when the Power's technicians are destroying Earth's natural shields–accelerated by the HAARP experiments upon the ionosphere. Intensified solar activity also places their satellites and space probes at greater risk, as it does their secret outposts upon the Moon and Mars. Let us say that the Sun's aberrant behavior at this crucial time in their celestial maneuvers is an absolute deterrent to the successful implementation of this, the final phase of the Power's schematic designs for Nebiru and Earth.

From our viewpoint, Ra's ecstatic fire is a spectacle of indescribable beauty. It is a celestial light show of untold brilliance; it is Spirit unfolding–Divinity in motion. Here is the material expression of light over darkness. Let it serve as a confirmation (for those who still need reassurance) of the eternal wisdom of Prime Creator…the manifestation of the God force that moves the Universe. You are privileged, observers of the universal principals of cause and effect, the ascending nature of Spirit and celestial evolution as they are being played out in the fields of three-dimensional reality.

For the beings of Sirius who are committed to serving you during this time of transition, it is a rare opportunity to experience the intensity of extreme emotion, for we are not as you. We are not capable of your range of emotions…and yet we can feel this.

**We can feel the fire.**

*        *        *

Let us analyze the transformative events occurring within the body of Ra. Know that periods of increased solar activity can be identified in physical terms and you now have the technology to measure the alternating energies of the Sun.

As we have suggested, solar flares are the physical expressions of the Deity's release of built-up energy in the auric field. These are experienced throughout the body of the solar system as release and renewal...**a letting go of Ages.**

To the pragmatic scientist, they are categorized as celestial nuclear explosions, which result in intensified bombardment of your planet from cosmic rays, gamma rays, x-rays, infra-red rays, ultraviolet rays, microwave and down to the low end of the electromagnetic spectrum, where radio waves are registered.

With the release of this pent-up energy, other planetary bodies of your solar system are being blasted with increases of solar energy...as is Earth. Knowing what you do about the interaction of celestial bodies in the heavens, you may wish to consider how these dynamics affect your sister planets and how those alterations affect the moods, energies and vibrations of human beings and animals upon the Earth. The rocks and mineral kingdom are no different; they hold within their essence the most ancient of all Earth memories and they keep the records of Ra's shifting energies from the beginning of Earth time.

Jupiter, the Great Liberator, plays a particularly significant role for humankind in this phase. Many of you, sympathetic with the Jupiterian vibration, were deeply affected by that planet's metamorphosis in 1994, when deep space bombardment of Jupiter caused a cosmic wave to wash over Gaia, and those of you who can feel these shifts sensed the transition.

We look upon these cosmic waves as triggers of your transmutational experience and we suggest that what is coming in from the Sun and the planets of its greater being is a natural part of your process.

The propaganda has you believing that the Sun's rays will harm you. We assert that the most imminent danger comes not from the Sun, but from those ionospheric heaters–the HAARP Project and its sister facilities–whose disturbance of the ionospheric layer actually causes mutation of the energy transfer coming into Earth orbit.

Enter NASA and its partner organizations, those intent upon the conquest and domination of space. We have intimated that the dramatic increase in radiation and these colossal solar explosions are hardly viewed as 'wondrous' events by the inventors of the satellite communication systems surrounding your planet. Violent solar flares disrupt the mechanisms of surveillance. They interfere with radio communications networks; they reek havoc upon the secret technologies of the hidden space program and its anti-gravity technologies; they interfere with covert activities taking place on the Moon and Mars and destroy the grid.

Moreover, surges in radio wave frequencies can easily disrupt and override the instruments of mass mood manipulation being used to entrain the world population. They can interfere with subliminal sound tracks in the Internet, disabling the mechanisms that are creating drug-like addiction to the Net and apathetic, hypnotic behaviors in the children.

Given what we have told you about electromagnetic frequencies and their applications in mood control, it should be reasonable to deduce that the Sun's heightened energy release is directly involved in breaking down the artificial controls that have been placed upon you. This is an important consideration, for it empowers you with the understanding that your Solar Deity is breaking the electromagnetic chains around you. How that occurs should, by now, make sense to you.

Validating this theory, NASA research teams report that with the advent of SOHO they are able to register and record sound wave emissions from the Sun's core. This little bit of information is highly significant, given our prior discussions of sound and frequency–of resonance–for it suggests that the teams are studying and attempting to record (and inevitably **control**) the soul music of Ra.

They claim that by measuring the sound waves emanating from the Sun's center to its outer body, SOHO can locate the regions of the solar body that are the most explosive, just as it can be used to identify where the most notable frequency variations are occurring. By measuring the sound waves emanating out from the Sun's center, SOHO recently detected subtle alterations in the Sun's physical form—an unfathomable measure!

Allowing this information to seep into your consciousness, you may realize that our galactic overview of current events in the material universe is not as 'far out' as it may seem. To record the sound waves emanating from the center of the Sun and use the data to measure how that sound alters its mass is an awesome undertaking. Do you ask yourselves why the government teams are involved in this aspect of solar research? One need not strain the imagination to imagine what might be the desired outcome of such studies.

We believe that the SOHO project and the intent behind it can serve to validate our teachings regarding sound and celestial harmonics, planetary resonance and the potential application of sound frequencies as a means to alter matter and human emotional fields. If nothing else, it provides you with a grounded base from which to investigate further the Secret Government's obsession with celestial sounds.

There is, of course, the spiritual aspect, which their science inevitably overlooks. It denies the consciousness of matter and energy; it does not consider the Sun or any other planetary being as a conscious, self-aware entity which thinks, feels, acts and reacts. In the process of measuring, analyzing and recording the Sun's changing fields, the government teams do not, for a moment, consider that this is **Deity**. Your brilliant Sun, great glowing fire, is exploding in spiritual ecstasy, in anticipation of what lies ahead and that they cannot measure—for neither do they understand nor believe in Divinity.

Therefore, trust the Sun. It is a supreme manifestation of All-That-Is, a fully conscious light being. It is aware of the universal forces of change and resistance; it is assisting in your evolution and Gaia's rebirth.

Some of you still await the Messiah, others ask if a savior will appear before humanity or if it will be extraterrestrials who are going to save you. Soon you will realize the perfection of the Divine Plan and how, despite appearances, everything that is occurring now is simply the manifestation of consciousness reaching higher. It will dissolve your terror of the unknown and bring you to the joyous light of discovery. There you will cast the rays of Spirit into your darkest fears, only to realize that they were merely shadows of a veil that has fallen away forever.

We suggest that you look to your Sun to know the true design of cosmic intervention. Perhaps it is time that you contemplate the Deity with renewed reverence, celebrating his awesome energy and the impact these emanations have had upon the evolution of the blue-green planet. Perhaps the time has come that you observe the sunrise with a new vision of its meaning in your lives and the knowing that this great glowing body is consciously preparing the way of your evolution—removing the obstacles of dark design from your path.

The government teams would block the Sun's light, so great is their desire to deter you. Their sinister bands of chemical clouds are proliferating everywhere above you, over the cities and urban regions where human beings congregate. A massive operation has taken wing, spanning the entire globe, and it being actively carried out, right over your heads!

When, we wonder, will you notice that the clear blue skies of Earth are beginning to turn murky and gray?

*         *         *

The question of *chemtrails*, the deliberate spraying of chemical cloud-generating substances over target areas of your globe, is slowly coming into public awareness. Although the governments boldly deny such overt activity against the citizenry, many of you are first-hand witness to the spraying of the skies. Other alert individuals have been photographing these mysterious flying trail makers and more of you are now sharing the information via your communications networks and public gatherings, as you become less fearful of speaking out against the Power.

We commend you for your courage, your vision and your love of freedom, for these are the higher aspects of your being 'human'.

Not all souls entering the physical realms choose the self-sacrificing road that leads to a lifetime search for truth and justice. You are the spirit warriors of the new millennium and you know you have chosen a difficult assignment in this incarnation, since standing up for the human race and all the living beings of your world makes you an annoyance to the Power.

Will you be thrown off your path by the threat of reprisal or will you insist, determined to facilitate the healing process while breaking down the walls of mainstream resistance?

Always remember that your security lies in the collective. Your sheer numbers and your focused intent are the determining factors that can swing the pendulum of power back to the people. Above all, your willingness to face fear rather than hide from it empowers you to move beyond the roadblocks that have been placed in front of you. United, you move forward as an unstoppable force, for the power of human determination is unlimited when you are working for the good of the All.

We believe that there has never been a more urgent need for humankind's resurrection than now, and we remind you that you are the trumpeters who have come to sound the wake-up call of the entire human race. Your rebellion and global outcry are needed if you are to spread the word to all those who do not yet have the will–or the awareness–to fight along side of you.

For those who are still unfamiliar with the spraying of the lower atmosphere–those reprehensible acts against humanity–we assure you that the appearance of latticed cloud-webs in your skies is every bit as deliberate as it is deadly. You must lift your gaze to observe what is happening there, rather than bury your worried heads in the sands of hopeless resignation.

The massive spraying of highly toxic materials in the lower atmosphere serves (the Power) a variety of purposes. One is directly related to the global management campaign intent upon reducing the populations of Planet Earth by imposing super strains of lethal bacterial and viral agents to sicken and kill targeted segments of the species. Quite simply, they have been creating the super viruses in their underground laboratories for more than fifty years and they believe that now is the time to put them to use on the grand scale.

Didn't you wonder if the lethal super viruses being concocted in the underground would one day be unleashed upon your world? Or were you lured into believing that biological warfare would somehow never touch your lives? We remind you of the AIDS and Ebola viruses, laboratory-engineered super strains that were originally inflicted upon the 'undesirable' and 'expendable' segments of the global population and have now permeated the globe. Others are constantly being tested at various outposts of the planet and we assure you that many more are on the way up to the surface in the very near future.

Killing off the 'undesirable elements' of society is no longer the primary goal of the designers of biological warfare. Neither is it the creation of new ways of destroying 'the enemy', however convincingly you have been sold such inhumane justifications for the taking of human lives.

No, what is behind the biological war against humankind is a well-planned global campaign designed to bring the runaway population explosion to a halt, while reshaping the survival conditions of those who remain. This will peak during the Desert Days, at which time vast populations will struggle just to stay alive, fighting for food and your ultimate resource: water. This has already begun, there amongst those remote third world populations so far from your world that their famine and suffering don't directly interfere with your dinner hour...or rouse you from the comfort zone.

Somehow, you believe that it can never happen to you.

That your own governments would spray you with deadly biochemical, viral and bacterial agents is something few people will ever accept as even a remotely possible reality. Yet, denial doesn't make this go away. Your fear and rejection of such potential acts do not alter the outcome, other than to intensify it. Only your awareness and public outrage–your Voice–can send the top guns back into their hangers.

If you need proof, go and gather it, for it can be identified in the gelatinous strings of toxic fall-out that stick to the leaves and petals of your gardens, the walls of your homes and the rooftops.

**They adhere to your lungs and cell walls as well.**

To elaborate this aspect of the spraying of chemicals in the atmosphere, however, is not our purpose here. We intend to discuss this and other conspiracies being perpetrated against you at length in later transmissions, which will begin upon completion of this emerging manuscript, *Atlantis Rising.*

For the moment, it is more relevant that we analyze the primary motivation behind chemtrail spraying, which has, as its intended objective, the creation of temporary, artificial barriers to shield against increasing solar radiation, while their ionospheric heaters tamper with specific regions of Earth's outer atmosphere. What is of importance here is that you understand how the creation of these cirrus-like cloud layers and the strange patterns being designed by the flying craft that emit them is part of an extensive program that has, at its fulcrum point, the HAARP Project and the exacerbation of Earth's natural frequencies. They are directly related.

As the technicians of doom continue their relentless manipulation of the ionospheric layer, sending unfathomable charges into the protective shield of Earth's outer body, harmful emanations from the Sun are no longer being adequately filtered or bounced back into space. Massive radiation pouring through the ionosphere is destroying the balance that was once held in the cosmic relationship of the Sun with the Earth.

The Power knows they have taken you to the brink of disaster, for they are teetering there, alongside of you. Yet, their all-consuming drive to reach resonance point overrides their concerns about the weakening of the shield and the destruction of Earth's aura. They are wild experimenters, blinded by their quest, for they believe they have found the way to achieve their ultimate objective—now, just as 'time' is running out.

Common sense will not deter them. Although they are well aware of the ramifications of such mindless invasion of Earth's sovereignty, they blast away, raising the ceiling of the ionosphere and gambling on the planet's ability to withstand and resist the forces of the Cosmos long enough for them to achieve their desperate goal.

One of their inadequate strategies to shield the planet from excessive solar radiation while they fry the natural barrier comes in the design of these haze-inducing patterns you now see scratched into the skies over your inner cities and rural fields. The chemical cocktail being sprayed overhead is supposed to hold up as a reflective screen against the radiation, scattering and deflecting some of more dangerous rays that are now penetrating Earth's aura and raining down upon you.

Of the strange designs that are being drawn overhead (the X's, numbers grids), know that these serve as target markers for their satellite surveillance equipment, indicating with eerie precision the quadrants that are primed for the gigawatt blasts of their atmospheric cookers.

Are you beginning to see the global picture?

Now...given what we have told you of HAARP and the Secret Government's deliberate alteration of the ionospheric layer of Earth's atmosphere, is it any wonder that there is a flurry of investigation into the potential manifestations of an unprecedented increase in solar eruptions?

Consider what the Sun's hyperactivity now, at this crisis point in the Annunaki's game plan, might mean to the playing out of events upon Earth and Nebiru. With what is in store in terms of solar force and its manifestations, it is becoming increasingly apparent that there is a potential turn-about for the Power. Reading the celestial messages, one can see the signs that their desperate survival plan is soon to fall apart.

Those satellite networks and surveillance equipment that now proliferate in space and the Earth environment are totally vulnerable to fluctuations in the Sun's ejections and can easily be knocked out of orbit and sent spinning off into outer space. Covert activities on the Moon and Mars will so be adversely affected. Neither will any human colonies in space survive the additional radiation raining out through the solar system. Indeed, the entire space project will potentially come to a halt in the last days of the ascension, and that is of particular significance to those of you who ask the question: "how can the Secret Government be stopped?"

As we have suggested, knocking out these technologies would wipe out their mind control methodologies as well, for disturbance in radio transmissions would interrupt (if not alter) any deliberate entrainment pulses or devices. Would it not be ironic if the Sun, great Deity of Light, were to simply switch the imposed frequencies of the controllers to a level that would enhance and empower the human spirit—rather than hinder it?

Know that a percentage of the damaging electromagnetic frequencies being beamed from the HAARP facility into the ionosphere hit the shield and bounce back to the lower atmosphere of Earth. When these ELF waves are reflected back at you, they penetrate your bodies, the waters and soil. They are experienced by the animals, the plants and mineral kingdoms of your world.

They penetrate past the surface and into the underground as well, creating disturbance **at every level.**

*          *          *

Rest assured that the devastating testing being conducted in your outer atmosphere cannot withstand huge increments of solar wind blowing through the ionospheric layer. The danger of these mad experiments at a time when Ra is unleashing such exceptional vibrations into the solar system is far greater for the life forms of your planet than even the Power can predict, for they are unaware of the effects of such celestial manipulations and they are ignorant of the Sun's overriding force fields. Yet, HAARP continues unceasingly, for the clocks of the Secret Government are counting down the hours that remain before you break free of their grasp, and their hopes of saving Nebiru slip away along with you.

It is not unthinkable that the unleashing of such forces could cause a switch-back reverse energy flow into the antennae of Alaska, traveling down their electromagnetic flow path and crashing into the HAARP plant with the force of ten million lightning bolts. Such a cosmic twist of fate could forever change the Alaskan landscape, obliterating all life and dramatically altering Earth geography as far east as the Canadian highlands, to the western icelands of Siberia and the seas and glacial masses in between.

**Such was the true fate of Atlantis.**

The alchemists of Akkaeneset's team, empowered by the Annunaki to explore all the possibilities that could emerge from the harnessing of Earth's geophysical properties, advanced the Annunaki's theory that reaching the resonance point of Gaia could potentially hold Nebiru (then in its phase of traversing your solar system) in Ra's orbit. The idea was essentially seeded by Akkaeneset, the time traveler, and elaborated upon in the laboratories of his design. His observation and experiments with the Atlanteans' mindlight generators and their interaction with Earth consciousness convinced him that non-sympathetic planets could be entrained to communicate vibrationally.

He imagined a form of psychic cording between Nebiru and Earth, and how the vibrational body of one could reach resonance with the other—thereby connecting with that body, overcoming the physical improbabilities involved in moving such a massive being through such incredible distances in material space.

The Annunaki believed they had found the answer to their existential dilemma. Akkaeneset's plan could work. There could be a way to reel Nebiru through some sort of multidimensional cord and bring it into a fixed orbit, if only Earth could be made to vibrate in resonance with their home planet. Fortunately, it didn't work then, and isn't working now.

Pushing Earth's energies to the limit, the Atlantean technicians created just such a switch-back energy reversal, drawing back down upon them the devastating forces of celestial disturbance which resulted from their resonance detonators. In the flash of an instant, all was annihilated.

Atlantis died—but not the hopes of the Annunaki, whose experience of the unleashed energies there was one of confirmation that, refined, the experiment could work.

That is the true design of HAARP and all the support technology—the pulling of Nebiru back into your solar system in time for ascension. And now, 13,000 Earth years later, when you are about to slip out of the material realm and beyond their reach forever, they are desperate to make it work. They are desperate to cling to you, to follow you through the tunnel…to survive.

After hundreds of thousands of years of attachment to Earth, they no longer know how to exist without you. They don't believe they can; they don't want to let go of you. Yet, taken to fruition, their very survival scheme would destroy you. They are entwined in the rope of human history—a karmic knot that ties them to you from your inception.

What you must ask yourselves is this: can you, seed of the Light Ones of the Universe, forgive the dark warriors?

It is important to your spiritual evolution that you carry no resentment or rage in your souls as you move towards the light of your heightened experience. As you seek to move beyond the extreme duality and polar conflict of your existing reality, be careful not to entrap yourselves in victim consciousness, for the forces of which we speak all bring you to the threshold. The Annunaki, their descendants and their brokers of power serve you, for throughout your history they have taught humankind about obedience versus sovereignty, about ego consciousness versus heart centeredness and, most significantly, about the liberating nature of forgiveness. This may just be your greatest challenge as you approach the new horizon, as it is by far one of the greatest lessons of existence.

As for the Annunaki…imagine. They have gone so far and come so near but still they are 'nowhere'. They are clutching and yet slipping and falling away, ever closer to the grey zone of non-existence. In clinging to you, they suffocate you—their hope. And now, as they feel the pulse right at their fingertips, the Sun is throwing them off course, breaking it all down.

That may help you to understand why the Annunaki act as they do; it may help you to dissolve the fear mechanisms and your rage, the food upon which they feed.

Your love is the key to your liberation.

**Love always is.**

# Chapter 11

## Subterranean Worlds

Let us not ignore Earth's underground, for there is much to tell about the below of your world and so much you need to know about its evolutionary progress. There are many layers, many worlds beyond your field of vision. Much is deliberately hidden there, too, far from the probing eyes of the curious and a lot more than the mere knowledge of the Government's secret underground cities and bases is beginning to surface now, as your excited Solar Deity illuminates the path of humankind's ascension...and Atlantis rises in your memory.

As you reach beyond the outer limits of your 'known' world, you discover life everywhere just beyond your grasp, there where the Earth establishment's biological formulas simply don't apply and life manages to find its way. This is the wonder of Prime Creator, who brings to life the most unlikely settings in the Universe. For all of us, sparks of the Divine, it is the wonder of being part of it all and being 'all of it' at the same time!

Conservative biologists cling to their conviction that life, as any other than the most elementary of forms, cannot exist without some degree of sunlight–excluding the possibility of living beings surviving in the underground. They confine Earth's boundless biological pool to the habitats of the surface world–their infinite living laboratory–yet, millions of species have yet to be detected, so vast is bio-diversity upon your planet.

In the black darkness of the Marianas Trench, so far below sea level that sunlight cannot penetrate its inky depths, hundreds of thousands of

135

spectacular species thrive, undisturbed–the majority of which still await discovery. Yet, most establishment thinkers still insist upon the existence of visible light as an absolute requirement for life to exist in the earth zone…and beyond.

We wish to state emphatically that the mere absence of the visible light of Ra does not exclude the presence of life, and we suggest that the time has come that you release yourselves from this prejudice.

It is enough to investigate the deep of your great oceans to know that unique and yet undiscovered life forms do indeed proliferate in the sunless environments of Planet Earth. Remember that the range of visible light is but a fraction of the electromagnetic spectrum. So are the life forms that require that light but a fraction of those which populate the material realm. Others thrive upon emanations of the high and low ends of the electromagnetic spectrum; these are the biological life forms of the 'in-vis-ible' light.

There is no limit to the abundance of life (in all its myriad forms) lying just outside your awareness. Only your restrained imagination prevents you from realizing that everywhere life abounds: in and above your surface world; in the ethers; in the dense rocks and minerals; out in space; in the darkness and the light.

We suggest that those who refuse to consider even a possibility of life in the underground or upon the planets of remote galaxies are those who believe in a finite approach to an infinite Universe. To try to contain the wonders of creation in some pre-conceived formula of proper Earth biology, or to believe that, in a Universe of billions of stars, one singular planet orbiting one singular star could possibly enjoy all of the elemental requirements for life to exist is, at the very least, self-serving and confining.

Those of other worlds are incredulous over how your race denies the obvious–that the chemical elements which comprise All-That-Is, as well as the conscious spark which 'ignites' them, exist not only upon your planet but **everywhere**, throughout the Universe, forming in an infinite range of combinations to create the superb diversity of life that defines the very nature of the Cosmos.

Despite the vastness of that diversity, there is a sameness to all life, for all beings are conscious manifestations of the primal thought of the Creator. This is an aspect that we must never overlook in our exploration of other worlds, beings and civilizations, as we examine how the exchange amongst us affects the Universe, as well as our individual experience.

Still in denial over any possibilities that fall outside of the established formulas of the biologists—those 'scientific' analysts determined to dissect the miracles of Prime Creator—humankind continually attempts to define the boundaries of Gaian bio-diversity. Yet, unknown species are being discovered almost every day, in the deep oceans and in the deserts, the jungles and the icelands. Always adapting, always finding ways to survive, always defying the limitations of dogmatic thought: this is the nature of life on Earth, as it is throughout the heavens!

Know, too, that as time begins to warp in on you—the tears in the three-dimensional framework are bringing forth prehistoric creatures, supposedly extinct bacterial forms and mutants from the so-called 'future'. These will soon move from legend, myth and science fiction to the foreground of human discovery, where they will then be poked, burned and 'anatomized' in the name of scientific analysis.

We are telling you that life abounds at all levels of existence: in every environment, in one form or another…in simultaneous time. The material universe is seething with it; the multidimensional realms are pure consciousness. It is above, around and below you. It is within. And, although most of the human race still believes that yours is the only planet of life in the Cosmos—positioning you as the Masters of the Universe—we assure you that you are not necessarily perceived as such by the countless billions of thinking, conscious creatures that live along side of you: upon and within the Earth, throughout the multidimensional Universe and in the ethers.

Therefore, we ask that you allow yourselves to envision at least a possibility that life could also exist in the underground, where before you may have only imagined slime and hellish phantoms...or nothing more than steaming rocks and a vaporous void. Perhaps a snake or reptile has slithered across the screen of your conscious imaginings of such a world, but few of you readily accept the idea that contemporary societies of thinking, productive and highly-evolved beings may actually thrive in the sun-deprived world below.

Yet, it is so. For untold millennia, the inner plains of your planet have hosted quite remarkable colonies of exquisite plant and animal species, some of whom were your long-forgotten human ancestors of Atlantis.

The greater body of natives, living in the highly populated coastal region of the continent, perished with the last great ice age, the closing of the second cycle of Atlantis. A substantial number of mountain dwellers, however, survived by taking refuge in the warmth of Gaia's inner body–for upon the continent of Atlantis were located numerous passageways into the deep inner lands of your planet.

Like many beings throughout the Cosmos, your great ancestors' migrations into the 'cave lands' were initially intended as a temporary reprieve–a matter of waiting out the cataclysmic events at the surface from the safe haven of the planet's protective inner being. They trusted that there they would find protection and that the way of survival would be shown them, especially since the frozen surface had become an absolutely inhospitable reality...and death was certain for those who remained above. There was, for all intents and purposes, nowhere else to turn. However, as they journeyed inward, many of the surface evacuees realized that they'd reached a terrestrial paradise–as if life in the often harsh conditions of the surface had merely served as a testing ground from which they had graduated and, in a sense, 'gone to heaven'.

There, in the rich underground of the continent, the Atlantean settlers found all the geophysical elements necessary to survive the freezing of the continent and more. Inner Earth was warm and lush, and as they penetrated deeper they found, to their amazement, an abundance of water: first streams and then rivers, which eventually led them to the shores of a great sea, bearing some very unusual forms of life.

They learned quickly how to adapt to the difficulties of their new home by studying and interacting with the species of the underground. Of these, there were sources of food, monitors of the other world, light bearers and scavengers. All were respected for their role in the perfect balance of the ecosystems. The second cycle Atlanteans, who had the utmost respect for all the living beings of Earth, were non-invasive newcomers to the underground and that respectful approach aided their acclimatization.

Consider, now, that by the end of the second cycle, the Atlantean civilization had attained technological sophistication. Isn't it plausible that they might have mastered technology to a point that enabled them to enjoy lighting, climate control and other modern comforts, such as those that you have created since the turn of the 20th century—a mere one hundred years in linear time?

Our telling you that generations of second cycle Atlanteans built complex energy networks and extensive artificial lighting (with which they successfully grew abundant food supplies) deep within the Earth may test your credibility...but it shouldn't, for it is no greater an accomplishment than your own extraordinary technological advancement...in far less time. To this day, hydroponic agriculture, growth-stimulated with alternative lighting, furnishes over 80% of the food required to sustain entire populations—all vegetarian—in the underground.

The mindlight generator network of the Last Generation of third cycle Atlanteans is only one example of the potential technology that would be required to create such subterranean power plants. Your contemporary engineers would be capable of inventing far more sophisticated solutions than those they are designing for the subsurface military stations, were they assigned the task of powering the deep, inner world with energy. Such designs would, by necessity, fall under the category of 'free energy' systems, ecologically-sound sources of energy that involve recycling waste and harnessing the winds and waters of Gaia to create light and other expressions of energy. These methods are available to you now, **if only the Power would place Earth ecology over profit and greed.**

If you just imagine the last one hundred years of progress and your technological achievements as a race, your resistance to these ideas may just yield to the wonder of such possibilities.

*     *     *

Of wondrous possibilities, we wish to speak to you now of an Utopian land of beauty and light—one that, unbeknownst to most of the human race, actually exists in Earth's contemporary physical reality.

In the deep inner world of Gaia, there lives a bustling, thriving civilization of highly evolved beings—descendants of the first Atlantean colonizers of the underground. Protected from the geophysical disturbance and upheaval that has swept your surface world for so many millions of years, the Atlanteans not only survived the last great Ice Age, but went on to create a superb world in the womb of the Earth Mother...a land of the yin vibration. A land known as **Agharta.**

The idea of a great underground civilization is no whimsical hypothesis. The world of Agharta and its cultural center, Shamballah, are well known to studied Buddhists and Tibetan lamas, and many are the mystics and visionaries who have 'seen' these lands and traveled there in astral body.

The fortunate and the chosen of your spirit leaders regularly visit there in physical form. Theirs is an extensive knowledge of the highly evolved world of the inner Earth, for they are frequent visitors to Shamballah, where they receive guidance and direction to bring back to the surface from the priests of the White Brotherhood presiding in this realm. Sages of many epochs have brought through the wisdom and brilliance of the idyllic civilization that flourishes below and the knowledge sits in your collective consciousness, awaiting recognition.

Throughout Earth time, diverse civilizations have interacted with these Atlantean super beings, for there are still tunnel openings at various points on the planet and there have been visitations from the Aghartans at various crucial points in 'surface time'. At pivotal moments in Earth's history, select societies, such as the Lemurians, Tibetans, the Maya, ancient Egyptians, the Druids and Etruscans were visited by Aghartan spirit leaders, who brought their wisdom to the surface to assist the souls transiting the outer world and to serve Gaia's higher purpose.

Of these, the Tibetans, many of whom are the reincarnated souls of the Atlanteans of the second cycle or direct descendants of the third cycle Atlanteans, had open contact until the middle of your last century, when the Boddhisattva, Dalai Lama, was forced to flee those sacred lands forever. The Tibetan portal in the spiritual vortex of Lhasa was sealed with his departure, to be replaced with one that extends from India through to the base of Mt. Kailas, and it is from here that journeys to Shamballah are still embarked upon by select Tibetan leaders—those who have been chosen to serve as messengers.

Other passageways into the deep inner lands of Agharta exist at key points of Planet Earth, but all are highly guarded—for they are the bridges between the outer and inner worlds, and that link renders the uncontaminated inner environments extremely vulnerable to all forms of human pollution and cosmic radiation.

While humanity's devastation of the surface ecosystems continues to ravage and destroy Gaia's innate beauty, we can tell you that the subterranean environment has, until recently, remained relatively pure, free of the poisonous emissions and toxic waste that have been poured into surface ecosystems and out into the atmosphere. The very survival of these contained habitats depends upon successful management of all waste products and total communion with the elements. This has been successfully managed from the days of early Atlantean penetration into the below.

Unfortunately, with the Secret Government's thrusting exploitation of the subsurface layers, the perfect biosphere of inner Earth and the harmonious life of the people of Agharta are being disrupted. To date, the invading engineers have only managed to bore into the crust—still far from attaining access to Agharta. Yet, their violation of Gaia's skeletal formations is disturbing the natural balance there as well.

Garbage and emotional toxins produced from their machinations and dark intent line the tunnels of their growing underground military stations. These putrid waste products are penetrating the airways and the waters that lead to the inner world, which serve to sustain life, holding the ecosystem in balance and harmonious inter-dependency.

On-going nuclear testing in the below has taken its toll as well, and the fields of that radioactive waste have begun to seep past the boundaries that once protected the world within. There, where illness was once unknown, effects of radiation poisoning are now slowly beginning to manifest in the population. This aggressive intervention, the plundering of all natural resources and the destruction of the ecosystems, is destroying the harmony of these worlds, for **it is the heart that opens a space without violating it; power rips and tears it apart.**

*       *       *

"Ah!" you may be thinking, "… subterranean civilizations—how 'in the world' can the Speakers ask us to accept this as truth?" We understand that the very idea taxes you, for it is so difficult for star children to imagine such worlds. Therefore, we wish to explore briefly some of its primary elements in a rather simplistic manner, such that you may come away asking yourselves if it isn't indeed more plausible than you believe.

Of the microorganisms which have always thrived in the subterranean seas, some are photosynthetic—floating units of stored light that enter through the main portals at the north and south poles. Billions of these bioluminescent creatures, moving in singular body, bring light into Earth's inner waters, stimulating plant growth at the banks and in the sea bottom.

They form the basis of the food chain, just as they do in those oceans of your ice-covered regions, where solar light cannot penetrate the surface.

Photosynthetic marine microorganisms are not new to you; they have been studied and observed by marine biologists. What is overlooked by the establishment thinkers, those who ridicule your contemplation of life below, is that **Prime Creator knows how to bring light into dark corners**–just as you do. This is only one aspect of how the Divine manifests life in every breath, at every turn and deep into the uncharted worlds that exist beyond your awareness.

Bear in mind what we have told you of the infinite electromagnetic spectrum and remember that there are many other vibrations of solar radiation that can penetrate the top layers of Earth's crust and be received in the underground. Remember, too, that it is the light of Prime Creator that determines from where life will spring forth–it is not the visible ray alone that raises the blade of grass from its bed.

Despite our determination to expose you to the life that dwells within, we know that, for most, the conviction that life could not exist in the 'dark bowels' of your planet simply overrides the logic of such a possibility, as it does your faith in the Divine Architect. This blanket of dogmatic thought is so deeply seeded in the mass mind that it seems to obliterate almost all human curiosity regarding the possibility of anything surviving there, as it does the idea of an entire underground civilization which has evolved (in spiritual terms) much faster than yours.

We, too, worship the solar deities, so we do understand your perplexity over such states of existence. Since modern biology denies the possibilities of life without sunlight, you put away thoughts of underground civilizations as nonsense stories of the Jules Verne variety–stories that have been **deliberately seeded** that way in your conscious and subconscious minds. However, humanity's rejection of the mere idea of subterranean civilizations is, in a sense, rendered untenable by a number of very valid arguments:

It is based upon the scientific establishment's egocentric 'what we know about life' attitude—a fixed field of conceptions that does not allow for what they do **not** know about biological diversity and multidimensional constructs.

Very little of the exploration of inner Earth (neither current nor ancient) has been made public, and much of what is being delivered to you is deliberate misinformation.

It is biased by what the power elite do and do not want you to know about their covert activities in the below and to distract you from investigating their massive military bases, underground biological and chemical laboratories, their top secret operational bases—and Agharta.

It does not consider the various levels of technological know-how which exist throughout the Universe and across linear time, providing relatively simplistic solutions to the problems of lighting, food production, waste management and air quality in the underworld. It is colored by your fear of the 'dark'.

If you wish to develop a multidimensional perspective of your world and your place in the Universe, you are going to have to give serious contemplation not only to what goes on around you, or to that which lies above, in the canopy of celestial beings that forms your heavens. You will also need to consider the below, for the inner world of Gaia—its vast lands and the seas—are no less magnificent than those of the surface, once one's physical senses yield to the innate abilities of psychic perception and the loss of the Sun's direct light is accepted at the cellular level.

You have only to contemplate a toucan's rainbow beak or a field of daffodils to affirm your conviction that you could never live without the vibrancy of color and the warm luminescence of sunlit plains, as you have known these abstractions until now. Your world is imbued with the brightest hues of the visible spectrum; they fill your eyes with their brilliance and this, in turn, evokes emotion within you. It stimulates the senses.

Yet, we assure you that the beings who have evolved in the below do not suffer in any way the lack of sunlight; rather, they live far healthier and longer lives without the damaging effects of solar radiation! They have evolved to become much less dependent upon the five senses, for in the underworld much less information is received through the physical mechanisms: the eyes, ears, nose, tongue and skin. One's perceptions and biological processes are of a distinctly different nature than those of surface dwellers, but that does not make the subterranean experience of life any less significant or meaningful than yours.

We do assure you that, despite your subconscious rejection of a sunless world, there are aspects to life underground that are, in so many ways, much more beautiful and nurturing than those you have created upon the surface.

Look about you and you will surely agree that there is much work to be done in the healing of Planet Earth. You are witness to the yielding of the last untainted habitats to the destructive hand of man; you suffer the heat and sterility of cement and steel where once green pastures cooled your souls and spoke to you of halcyon days and Gaia's inner peace. Even your crystalline turquoise skies are becoming gray and hazy, as the color slowly drains from the picture of Earth's most breathtaking landscapes.

Distracted by the happenings of your daily lives and global events, you simply haven't bothered to look too deeply into the question of what goes on just outside the camera's field of vision. With what you know about the globe and your penetration of its farthest reaches, there has been little reason to believe that there is much left to discover about your own planet. Seeing beyond the limitations of common belief structures—the 'what we know' syndrome of the establishment—requires inspiration, a compelling desire to understand the true workings of your world and, above all, the openness of mind required to observe things as they really are…as well as how they can be.

You realize that most of humanity simply defers to the dogma, for the masses are distracted by **appearances**. Most are passive reactionaries, moving along in a very unassertive manner until something upsets the status quo, and only then dealing with the momentary upset in order to re-establish the pace of their daily lives. As a result, it is easier for most just to pass over thoughts of new frontiers and untold possibilities, for it takes too much energy and can easily upset the apple cart.

Let us not forget that human passivity is stimulated by mind and mood manipulation technologies, which have been imposed upon you for so long that most of humanity cannot even remember free thought space. Such mechanisms have been in place and operative (at varying levels, in various moments) since the time the Annunaki first threw their electromagnetic net around your world...one hundred thousand Earth years ago.

Only the focused amongst you, those whose brilliance cuts like a laser through the density of human indifference, have had the courage and the vision to look past the stage set, questioning the true meaning of the longest running play in the history of human theater.

You, the rebels, have managed to hold your integrity, deflecting the covert waves of the mind engineers. You are swimming in the open seas, unafraid to dare...to challenge...to seek. We celebrate your strength and conviction.

To the rest we reaffirm that there is an entire world—a parallel reality—right there, beneath you...and that much of what is brought to the outer world by the spirit leaders who reach Shamballah reflects upon the human condition in most significant ways.

*    *    *

Although your understanding of life's potential fields of existence is extremely superficial (in a quite literal sense of the word), we assure you that throughout the universe of matter there exist many subterranean civilizations comprised of life forms of every imaginable shape and form...and many more of the 'unimaginable' variety. For many planets, such as Nebiru, life-supporting internal environments are more nourishing than those of above and, quite naturally, civilizations of compatible life forms have evolved in those habitats, protected from the often harsh conditions at the surface.

In the case of Nebiru, the planet's expulsion from Sirius and its ensuing journey through the cold galactic winter of space denies it the vitality of solar energy. This is quite an extraordinary situation in celestial mechanics. The internal chemistry of that planet body must therefore be supplanted for thousands of years by cosmic emanations and alternative energy supplies which assure the planet's survival, as it bounces from one solar system to the other, gathering and storing the resources and solar energy available during its passage through the respective solar fields.

The material universe is host to innumerable planets unsuitable for life upon the surface, whose inner beings are nonetheless teeming with complex civilizations, comprised of intelligent life and a vast diversity of biological creatures and forms. Some, like those in the underground communities of Mars and Nebiru, are a sort of relocation project of populations forced to evacuate their surface civilizations and re-establish themselves below ground–for reasons not unlike those which you fear will occur on Earth, such as devastating radiation, the destruction of the atmosphere and deep space bombardment.

For the Nebiruans, surface survival is no longer possible, as we have described in an earlier passage. What remains of their race is a declining civilization in the Nebiruan underworld, a sub-culture of Annunaki technicians in the Martian laboratories and a collection of hybrid humans descended from the time of their genetic interbreeding in the days of their intervention in Atlantis, back before the fall. They, the Annunaki lords who direct the Secret Government of Planet Earth, have never fully integrated with human civilization and they do stand apart, however disguised by their humanized forms and habitats. They are by far the most cold-blooded creatures of your world.

Other subterranean civilizations, like Agharta, co-exist as a parallel reality of a fully-populated surface race and it is often (but not necessarily) the case that the two worlds never interface. This is common knowledge to those of the Universe who are communicating with each other, and it is a mutual experience, for commerce and cultural exchange take place at countless stations in the galaxy…inside, above and upon innumerable planets.

You, the citizens of Gaia, are just momentarily 'out of the loop', but that is going to change very soon. Very soon, indeed.

In your quest to understand the enormity of All-That-Is—your desire to find your place as human beings in the multidimensional Universe—remember that life knows no limits. Consciousness cannot be classified to meet a finite set of criteria in which it can exist, for the designer, Prime Creator, is 'in-finite'. Ours is a Cosmos bursting with the desire to be…to live…and, like the blade of grass, it pushes past all confinement and restrictions, reaching forever for the Eternal Light. Therefore, as you come to the controversial question of life underground, come with thoughts of the 'possible'—there beyond what you are told to believe; there at the heart of what you know about creation—for we assure you that there are no limits…there are only possibilities.

From your perspective as surface dwellers of the Earth, you will soon recognize how life abounds in every direction: east, south, west, north, above, below and within the planet. Pray to the seven directions, celebrating all the spaces you have yet to explore and all the potential worlds awaiting your discovery…considering at least the possibility that the inner body of Gaia is just as vital and alive as is the 'within' of every human being.

Humanity's search for unknown lands and civilizations out in the galaxy and there, within the Earth, will yield far greater treasures than those carried off by those eager explorers who once sailed into the sunset to re-invent humanity. Remember, too, that it was only a very few hundred years ago that the authority decreed Earth to be a flat surface, and that venturing too far out upon the oceans would surely have meant falling off the edge of the world and into 'the great abyss'.

And so, we do acknowledge your difficulty with the very idea of subterranean civilizations and the forms life would take there and we appreciate that it is in some ways more difficult to accept than the existence of extraterrestrial life, for you identify with the stars. Your genetic roots are there.

Perhaps it is because the underworld is so close and yet so far from your awareness, but that is changing rapidly, as the Secret Government extends its reach into the below. Their rape of the underground is finally beginning to get your attention, no matter how cleverly they conceal their machinations. You merely need to dig a little deeper to uncover the secrets of Earth's inner world. There is a story there, waiting to be told.

We suggest you examine with greater interest the subsurface activities of your world governments. Your acceptance of our hypotheses regarding subterranean life will be made easier, once you investigate the documented evidence of underground cities. It is enough to simply enter into one such public environment, such as the underground of Montreal, and observe how entire communities can and do function below the surface.

Bear in mind that the architects of the covert coring of Earth don't necessarily want you to know what they're up to down there, just as they hide what they're into out in space. Yet, for those of you who have conducted a minimum of investigation, it is no secret that secret societies and control networks have already been established in a number of subterranean cities. There are squads of military personnel, medics, laboratory scientists; there are cooks, mechanics and laundry personnel; there are entire communities assigned to the underground.

It might strike you as extremely peculiar that while your governments are digging away at Earth's inner core, building miles and miles of tunnels, power stations and military bases in the underground, they still refuse to pronounce themselves on the grave state of your global environment. It is as if they are preparing the farewell exit when no one else has been told it is about time to go. Why aren't you hearing the story of their activities below? Moreover, who is being allowed access to the growing underground communities and what are they doing there?

What is most significant is the recurring aspect of renewed subterranean development during times of potential disaster upon the surface. It is the historical pattern not only of the human species, but of others in threatened habitats in space. We ask that you consider the Atlanteans' penetration of the underground as a natural and logical survival plan, no more unbelievable than the knowledge that below many of your capital cities are built many-layered 'research' centers, hospitals, luxury condominiums and food production facilities. They have effectively reproduced all the necessary life support systems required to comfortably house many thousands of key players in the global theater, in the event that another global catastrophe–such as the final destruction of Earth's atmosphere–might annihilate all life upon the surface. Know that you, the surface dwellers, have been deliberately kept in the dark about this for decades–since the unleashing of the atomic bomb, when full-scale penetration of the subterranean environment was given top priority by the governments of Power.

Once those emergency bases were established, the teams went on to develop far more complex infrastructures–fully operative cities–**places that you still believe do not exist**. There they go about their business of redesigning and ruling the Earth, unencumbered by your scrutiny, while humanity, distracted, scurries overhead.

Be aware. The global exploitation of subterranean ecosystems has inexorably altered the habitats of the underworld, and that which has been a perfectly self-sufficient biosphere for countless millennia–the remarkable civilization of Agharta–is no longer safe in the inner world of Gaia.

The Power's violent interference in the uncharted lands of the below is integrally part of the ecological crisis that you are experiencing upon the surface, for you know that all is connected and that all parts affect the whole. It is so vitally important that you understand the significance of their interference in the subterranean world, as well as their experiments in the upper atmosphere, for these regions of Earth are no less 'Gaia' than the trees and rivers of your precious surface landscapes.

If you consider the annihilation of the native peoples–such as those of the Americas, or the Aborigines of Australia–you will surely understand how the plague of modern civilizations infect, invade and destroy whole environments and species which formerly thrived in their isolated, uncontaminated eco-systems. So it has been with the infiltration of the underworld. As the invaders penetrate deeper into these uncharted lands, their massive drilling machines and explosives ripping apart the natural landscape, life is being blotted out, burned in the toxic invasion of its sacred spaces.

Let us not overlook the effect of their monstrous experiments: the genetically altered life forms that escaped (like the Chupacabras) or were simply left to survive there–or the killer viruses that are being concocted in the underground laboratories. These, too, are realities of your modern day, as they were in Atlantis, when the Annunaki trained the most obedient scientists of the Last Generation in the possible applications of genetic engineering and the technicians of *Hekkatl* (Atlantean headquarters of all underground biological research and genetic engineering) created strange new species to meet the specific needs of their masters.

Much was left behind then, to take its unnatural place in the evolutionary process of those worlds, and much more is being created now, far from the eyes of those who would, no doubt, find a way to shut it all down...if only they knew what absolute madness is being stirred up in the geneticists' cauldrons.

As all is interdependent, you can surmise how the destruction of the below is affecting the ecology of the surface. Therefore, we believe that it is extremely important for you to recognize how the world of inner Earth is altering the outer reality and how the imbalance being created on the planet affects your lives. Like no other time in human and planetary history, Gaia requires your absolute attention. She is calling out, trembling and storming around you–screaming to be heard!

Therefore, it is time that you become consciously aware of your world by observing with **eyes that see** what is actually happening within your range of vision. Ask of your guides to be shown only that which serves your higher purpose, and the inner eye will receive insights into those relevant aspects that lie just outside of the visible realm. This is what it is needed if you are to become fully conscious, multidimensional beings.

As you release yourselves from the blinding fear that has convinced you never to look into dark spaces–fear that has been programmed into you–you will see so much more clearly. Consider, too, that much of your conditioning regarding what lies below you is the product of religious indoctrination, for it is there that Hell has found its assigned location...there, in the underworld, the 'inferno' of the damned.

How can you help but visualize dark, frightful places and menacing creatures from the deep? They have been burned into your imagination of a world that lies below the surface...a dark, steaming cauldron where evil reigns. Yet, once you move beyond thinking that, somehow, looking will only frighten you more, you will realize what great power lies in exposing the darkness to the light of your brilliant, inquiring minds.

You will see what can no longer remain hidden from view, for it is there that you will 'un-earth' the knowledge needed to perform your true mission as lightworkers of the New Dawn.

We assure you that there is magnificence beyond your wildest dreams in the caves, grottoes, underground rivers and lakes of Mother Earth, just as there are dangers and polar forces creating the dynamic tensions that you know all too well above. Those of you who have reached the lands of Agharta in meditation and Wesak rites know of the beauty, for you have gazed upon the splendor and you have felt the vibration.

# Chapter 12

## The Forces of Light

Ours has been a clear provocation. We have called upon you to stand tall against the false gods and to speak out against the mechanisms of loveless power, for it is you who must initiate the process of disarming the dark ones by shining the light of knowledge into their hidden chambers. It is you who must perform that function, sharing those secrets with the awakening of your world. It is you who have come back to right the scales.

We have asked you to stand for Gaia, to become aware and involved in her process. We have called you to unity, reminding you of your purpose and of the power of the collective unconscious. We have incited you, pointing to the above and below of your world, so that you might expand your horizons beyond the boundaries that have been delineated for you upon the surface.

This, because we believe that you must recognize the pieces of the puzzle before you can understand how they will all fit together. To be most effective, you need first to observe the big picture, break it down into manageable bits and then, only then, will you be capable of putting it all back together.

Those of you who still fear opening Pandora's Box are going to be powerless in the wake of change. It is that unrelenting fear that takes your power, not the knowledge that will come flying out of that treasure chest…soaring far beyond its dark confinement.

The Light Ones of many realms have charted the way to the road paved by your soul, so you need never fear that you might be clutched from behind and dragged unwillingly into the shadows. As long as you, as conscious beings, intend that you refuse to be held in ignorance or be manipulated and controlled by the insipid dark force, nothing will impede the soul's journey. Only when you walk of your own will towards the inky vapors of the perilous night do you momentarily lose your direction and, even then, you eventually find your way back.

In the end, you see, there is only the one road–**the way home.**

You are being directed to uncover secrets that can no longer be kept from the citizens of Gaia, rebelling in unison against the actions being taken against you and the planet upon which you reside. To this end, know that you have the assistance of the Light Forces of the Universe at every juncture. Your spirit guides point you gently towards the pathways, but you exercise free will in deciding whether you will embark upon the journey or choose to cling to your inertia, afraid of change.

Angelic beings hover, spreading their great 'wings' around the whole of your race–loving energies that heal and forgive your errors, while celebrating your victories and your strength.

Gaia's own spirit guides are pointing the way, for no conscious being in the Universe is without the guidance of higher beings. Even your Sun–the Light Bearer, Ra–is working for you, knocking out the devices of control and helping to disintegrate the grid. So much light is being anchored upon the Earth and within you that, despite appearances, the dark side simply cannot hold its grip any longer.

The love that is pouring down from the heavens and your growing unification are melting the chains of your servitude and setting you free. Great waves of cosmic energy are being beamed to your Sun system from the far reaches of the galaxy, for Ra is a brilliant star and–just as Sirius–his is a magnificent light. The whole of the Universe is buzzing in anticipation of your imminent passage.

*　　　　　*　　　　　*

Never forget, however, that it is the light amongst you–that light which passes from heart to heart–that shines the way of your evolution. You are sparks of creation, the brilliance of All-That-Is. It is the love within you and your trust in the purpose of all creation that liberates you from ever doubting the meaning or the outcome of existence.

If you are fearful of the changes that are soon to occur, worried about the plight of the race and the future of the planet, or if you experience resentment of those who wish to shake you from your cages, then perhaps you might consider that the time has come to heal the lower vibrational centers of your being. As the intensity of your shifting solar family reaches new peaks, you will need to release those blocked energies, letting the waves flow through you and into the earth, where your fears can be purified and grounded.

It will be important to resolve your survival issues and center your consciousness in the heart. From a place of forgiveness and unconditional love, you will be capable of looking upon the perpetrators of ignorance and fear with forgiveness, for (in the end) they are too locked in survival mode to know any better.

If you consider their galactic circumstances, you may understand why they are so slow to evolve. Caught in the endless struggle, fighting extinction of their race and their planet, they have clung desperately to their material existence, knowing that at any time they could easily slip away into the emptiness of the gray zone. It is the only way they know how to exist.

They have taught this spiritless vision to their descendants, those upon Earth and others stationed in the inner worlds of Mars–instilling in them the primordial fear that there is nothing for them beyond the universe of matter.

*             *             *

Those of you who served the light in the Last Generation have returned to right the scales. You have confronted the dark force in many lifetimes, always in preparation of this moment. Most of you reincarnated at target points of the planet, in key civilizations where the story and the Wisdom would not be forgotten. You have lived in the Tibetan plains; you have walked in the peaks and valleys of the Andes. You have traveled the desert sands of Egypt; you have sailed the Mesopotamian seas. You have carried the story of Atlantis throughout the no-time and across the lands, keeping the knowledge of humankind's greatness alive.

You, who feel the Atlantean chord tugging at your memory, have crystallized again in Earth space, because you know how to help. We see you searching for ways to fill in the blank spaces and get on with the work that has called you back into physical reality, facing the karma of a lifetime you have catalogued, in your subconscious libraries, as a world in which you walked thirteen thousand Earth years ago.

We remind you that in the higher dimensions, there is no 'time'. As difficult it may still be for you to understand the no-time, we wish to make clear to you how all 'lifetimes' occur, in actuality, simultaneously. That is, what we have had to describe in linear terms—the past and the future—is, (in multidimensional terms) all part of the **now**. It is important to remind you that when we speak to you of history and of time, we do so because of the complexity of the no-time for those trapped in the illusion of time, as you have been until now.

Let us quote from earlier teachings, redefining to you the notion of the no-time, as we presented it in *The Cosmos of Soul*:

*Time as you experience it from within the confines of three-dimensional reality is a totally artificial framework. That is, your perception of time is based on a linear construct of some ambiguous past, an illusive, indefinable present and a future of projected outcomes that often cause you to be anxious and uncertain about your lives. In truth, most of your difficulties stem from your misconceptions about time, particularly now, at the turning of the millennium. You are beginning to attempt conscious awareness of the 'now' moment, of living it, but most of you are far from grasping that there exists nothing else.*

*This is understandable, for the experience of no-time is of a higher realm beyond your present capabilities, although you do touch upon it in your dream states and out-of-body experiences—there wherever you escape the sensate world. For this reason is it so essential to your spiritual unfolding that you explore your dream material, meditate, and develop your abilities to project yourselves out onto the astral. There lie the greatest opportunities to release from your limitations and drift in the sweet liberty of timeless awareness and body-less motion.*

*From the higher octaves, what you perceive as past, present and future is viewed as co-existential and simultaneous. This is absolutely incomprehensible from the three-dimensional viewpoint, for your history—your very race consciousness—has evolved around a model of linear time. Yet, if you can recognize the no-time of multidimensional reality (if even only intellectually), you can be freed from past nightmares or memories of better times, as well as futuristic inventions such as the impending apocalypse of doom.*

*In rediscovering your light selves, you begin to integrate the concept of soul consciousness creating and recreating itself in body, which you are currently moving through past and future hypotheses you perceive as real, fearful and fantastic happenings that you believe caused your life to be as it is, or 'some day' events to be lived in nebulous time, which lie always just outside of your reach. Paradoxically, the past-present-future illusion is so credible, so seemingly tangible, that it is unfathomable how time can exist in any other context.*

*As your lives are organized on that plane, you have needed the pseudo-structure of time-in-a-line, for it has pointed you, as a race, in the directions of the winds of change, both forward and back in your projection of the past and the memory of your future. And no one is going to convince you that a tomorrow of sunrise, a first cup of coffee, the office and the myriad activities of daily routine are mere figments of your imagination…yet we dare to emphasize that it is so. There is nothing but the moment.*

*That is the reality–the experience. Moments within moments, forever imprinting upon the matrix of Eternal Mind.*

These are the restraints imposed upon our communication, for, until you are freed from linear time, you are bound to it. That, in turn, binds us to those thought bubbles and it alters the message, as if, in passing through the dimensions, we must necessarily contradict ourselves in order to convey the essence of the experience in terms that can make sense to you.

We can tell you that all experience is simultaneous and that, in multi-dimensional terms, there are no past or future lives at all. All aspects of individual consciousness are merely sparks of the Great Flame–the unit, or soul essence, of the All.

**The spark is within every cell of your being; it is your essence–your godliness.**

Therefore, on some level that you have yet to understand, we ask you to consider that if you walked in Atlantis, you still exist there, and that your present world existed then, on the viewing screen of the no-time, where all experience is One. We invite you to give some thought to how Atlantis currently exists as a parallel reality, so close to you that you can slip in and out of that realm with incredible ease, although the actual 'going' there still eludes your conscious awareness.

Very soon, as the veil of three-dimensional limitation lifts from your vision, you will understand. You will recognize yourselves as the ancient Atlanteans, and you will realize how you are working from many realms to resolve the conflicting energies of the 'then' of your reality and the 'future' that lies before you.

Those of you who worked for the light of Atlantis took great care to prepare the way for the emergence of new civilizations. Your work was considerable, for you were anchoring the light in the physical reality, while weaving that consciousness through other dimensions. The Keepers of the

Crystals (those of the third cycle) stored the memory in the consciousness of the mineral kingdom, burying the codes in the crystal matrix and knowing that you would return to the caves to retrieve the Wisdom embedded there.

You know this. You know when you are accessing the knowledge in your work with crystal beings, for many of you were actually those who programmed them to begin with!

In the process of reincarnating, you come into physical reality at pre-determined moments of human evolution; from a multidimensional perspective, these can be best defined as 'designated points in the space-time continuum'. You do exit from the material reality constantly, although you are rarely aware of it. At any moment of your waking or sleeping experience, you may slip into parallel worlds in which you also exist and with which you hold resonance–for whatever experience your soul requires.

Often, you move in and out of your present reality to retrieve information or to experience a related sensation. Other times, you contribute to the probable realities that are constantly shifting those realms, fully participant in those other dimensions. In those 'moments' or 'spaces', you create a form of exchange or linkage between the two realms and it is the case that others from alternative realms can bleed into your space, resonating with you.

Those who have developed the ability to reach states of deep meditation or to consciously project themselves upon the astral are much more aware of this process. They are capable of willing themselves into a 'space' and experiencing it for a pre-determined purpose; they are gifted with the ability to assist from the higher dimensions, manifesting their intentions in physical reality. These are characteristic of time travelers such as Akkaeneset, whose extraterrestrial capabilities provided him with the understanding necessary to access these realms in full consciousness, while holding body in 3D. Unfortunately, all too often he appeared to work from the lower astral planes, embracing the shadow and giving it form in your world.

In death, or shall we say in passing from a physical lifetime, you are totally aware of your soul's projection—the multidimensionality of consciousness. Here you finally understand how resonance plays the keys of your existence, for you are drawn to those realms that are vibrationally synchronistic with your being. You realize how very remarkable and yet absolutely simple it is that the mere emission of a thought can create an entire world, and yet it is so. As the soul swims through the cosmic sea, it scintillates with the rhythm of certain waves, riding onto distant shores—across time, across space.

That, dear ones, defines who you are: where you come 'from', and where you are 'going'.

Now, as you approach a totally new experience (beyond the physical realm), you will no longer need to crystallize back into the restraints of the three-dimensional world you have known as Earth beings.

You knew this then and you know it still. You have come full circle.

As the Sun, Earth and the planets of your solar system prepare for the awesome experience of their passage, galactic beings of many worlds—of the universe of matter and beyond—are sending love to your realm. Those who resonate with Earth are working with tone, pitch and vibration to help you center the energies. The Galactic Federation is involved in assuring that the free will zone be honored, and that the universal laws of non-interventionism be upheld. Others, such as the Pleiadian Light Emissaries, are opening the multidimensional portals to assist in your passage. Lightworkers from worlds that you have yet to imagine are flooding the Gossamer Web with the brilliance of countless light beings from throughout the Universe.

We, the Speakers of the Sirian High Council, are linking with you, transmitting these teachings to those who are prepared to hear them, in order to help you reach into the collective well of your ancestral memory. There you can retrieve the knowledge of Atlantis...the ultimate story of human existence.

You are asked to take the first steps.

Free your minds of the prejudices that you have built around you, as if set concepts somehow protect you from danger. Explore the tales and ideals of others, especially those that defy the dogma. There you will often find nonsense and sometimes find great wisdom, but let that not deter you from listening. Through the heart, all is filtered and truth resounds.

Be daring. Remember that 'there is nothing to fear but fear itself', and trust that you can allow yourselves to hear the story of the dark warriors and how they take your power. You can investigate the abuse of your sovereignty by those of the Secret Government, learning more about the mechanisms used to hold you in obedience. You can look, unafraid to utter the names of the Annunaki or speak of their deeds and you can suggest alternatives without being segregated from your communities.

Do not be afraid to step out of the mould, for that is how leaders are born. It is your right to challenge the dogma and find new answers to the unsolved questions of your societies. By seeking out Truth in every aspect of your lives, you are acting in the full light of knowledge, serving as a member of the White Brotherhood.

Therefore, do not despair. The pendulum swings again and your star has the momentum—moving you to brilliance.

Dear Ones, of you we know with certainty one undeniable truth:

You came into your current 3D reality to serve as the catalysts of change that will help calm the fury and bring the inner sanctuaries and surface lands of Gaia back to center.

**Children of Atlantis, you came back to free the world.**

# *Epilogue*

We do not deny that your world is in grave condition and that, despite your hopes for a positive outcome, it often appears that the dark side is winning again, as it so seemed in Atlantis...but we see light there on Planet Earth. You are shining through. As great waves of love penetrate and destroy the grid, your brilliance traverses the cosmic network: the Gossamer Web of Light. More of you are awakening now and this process is accelerating as time begins to warp on you. You are tuning up for the celestial symphony, where all the Light Ones of the Universe are joining in chorus, celebrating the song of Ra.

No longer will the pounding of the master's drum beat out the rhythm of Earth's evolution.

There is such triumph in the human spirit, which shines through in times of cataclysm and crisis. As you rally to the call of the suffering, the pure love of Spirit pours through you, burning like lightning through the dark clouds of human turmoil. Rising above your personal concerns, you realize that those are your brothers and sisters buried below the ruins and drowning in the floodwaters. You run to each other's aid, embracing the weak and the wounded, and together you celebrate the One Heart: the emerging soul of humanity.

This is just such a time on Earth for, despite your growing fear and despair over the catastrophes now unfolding around you, you are moved in the knowing that you are still capable of placing others above your immediate interests...still capable of feeling. Your protective cloaks have become weighty and tiresome, and so you have begun to strip down to the basics, rediscovering the greatness of just **being human**.

United, you are working for the Mother, seeking solutions for Planet Earth, for she, too, seems to be drowning in the storm of human emotion.

Paradoxically, great disasters do also serve the highest good, although that may seem insignificant in the face of the pain and suffering of those caught in the wake of destruction. We believe that you, lightworkers of this Age, are capable of healing the deep wounds that have been inflicted upon Gaia. We are convinced of your ability to alter the intensity of your process and bring the planet through unscathed.

We believe in you, children of Atlantis.

We believe in you.

*　　　　*　　　　*

There are new challenges and some difficult times ahead of you, this we do not deny. You will be called upon to rise above your fear and show others the way, for this is the new dawn of the entire solar family–the birthing of Ra–and you are soon to know magnificence beyond your wildest imagination. You may choose to face great hardships and tremendous loss, or you may intend not to suffer **in any way whatsoever** the coming changes. This is a decision only you can make. When you realize that there is nothing to fear–not even death, your glorious transformation–then you can bring yourselves to Center to find the atoll in the midst of the violent waters.

If enough of you find that place, Gaia will reflect your trust and fearlessness and come through without fury.

You have only to recall the events of the New Year's Eve, to which some looked with fear and anxiety as the possible 'end' of the world, while around the globe humankind celebrated the turning of the clock–heralding the new millennium. Enough of you believed in the celebration, the peaceful convergence of the All, and you anticipated the joy and wonder of what lies ahead of you. You intended a positive global experience, and it was so. You created it.

You are capable of this every day of your lives.

We observe how you create challenges for yourselves, and how, in finding resolution, you give meaning to your existence. You find your purpose. Consider your many experiences of overcoming adversity and then moving forward in the light of your resolutions and you will realize that those are some of the most special moments of your lives. It is as if you need crisis, although you may not admit to it, for it is not easy to see beauty in pain ...especially when you have been taught and programmed to fear it so.

During easy times, when all is serene and undisturbed in your immediate world, complacency easily turns to boredom and soon you create crisis–however small, however insurmountable–from which you inevitably emerge victorious. It is the godliness within you that pushes you onward, always moving towards the light, and that, dear ones, is the Reason of all existence.

It is the return to All-That-Is, the infinite journey of a spark of divine consciousness which, having lurked in the shadows and danced in the sun, eventually finds its way home.

The road is as long as you are infinite.

You may encounter as many dark corners as you wish to create for yourselves, just as you can pave the way with the glitter of angels. The phantoms of your own design will never harm you, once you remember that you have embarked upon this long and wondrous voyage to know choice and free will and to bring that experience back to Source.

We have presented you with the dilemma, and now we call you to resolution–that you rebel against the controllers and **take back your power.** Release from the hold to re-establish yourselves: the free-willed, bright stars of Planet Earth. Gaia awaits your revolution–the overturning of all false masters–so that she can journey into the Fourth, healing the wounds and inconsonance of her final hours in the universe of matter.

We call you to unity, reminding you that you are sovereign beings, each with a time, a season and a rhythm–each with a song, a message and a reason.

Look around you. Everywhere the flower blooms, the bird still sings, life constantly breaks through and begins anew.

You are that flower...you are the song and the magic.

# *About the Channel*

A native of the San Francisco Bay Area, Patricia Cori has been immersed in the New Age Movement since its inception there in the early 1970s. She has utilized her clairvoyant abilities in healing and support work throughout her life, which has been dedicated in great part to the study of mysticism and philosophy, ancient civilizations, metaphysical healing, spirituality and extraterrestrial life.

A former Atlantean healer, she was drawn to working with crystals and color as the tools with which she felt the greatest resonance. In her crystal healing and pranic healing work, she focuses on releasing energy blocks and negative thought forms from the aura, restoring balance and joyousness in the Self, and often opening the individual to past life recall and out-of-body journeying. Energy balancing, in which she utilizes crystals and Tibetan singing bowls to resonate to the musical vibration of the body, revitalizes the electromagnetic energy fields, bringing the lines of force back into their natural alignment and the body's bio-resonance to a pure, tonal frequency which leads to good health and normalizes the aging process. Color therapy involves the application of color through full-spectrum lighting upon the etheric body, to bring healing on the mental, emotional, metabolic and physical levels.

As a dedicated teacher, Patricia has helped many realize their natural healing abilities, which are brought forth via intensive training in crystal healing and balancing of the body energies.

Patricia has lived in Italy since she emigrated to Rome in 1983, knowing that she had to take part in a mission...as she was instructed by her guides that she would have to help "burn a hole in the lead dome..." In 1995, she founded the LightWorks Association (a non-profit organization), one of the first Spirit centers to appear in the Eternal City, whose studios served as a healing center, school and the city's only New Age Library. She is a prominent figure in the New Age Movement, well-known on the lecture circuit–offering courses, seminars and workshops in England, the U.S, Thailand, Italy and Egypt on a vast range of topics, which reflect her broad knowledge of alternative methodology in healing and her conscious awareness of the Higher Knowledge. At the exclusive Thai Health Resort, Chiva Som, she is a returning Associate Healer and lecturer, teaching guests how to incorporate the Ancient Wisdom into their overall approach to healthier living.

She has been actively channeling the Speakers of the Sirian High Council (light beings from the sixth dimension) since her first visitation to the crop circles in 1996, and continues to lecture and write their messages for those who seek the wisdom.

Her first channeled book, *The Cosmos of Soul–A Wake-up Call for Humanity*, was released in October 2000 by Gateway Books, an imprint of Gill and Macmillan Publishers (Ireland).

To learn more about her lectures, seminars and courses, you can contact Patricia at:

patcori@tiscalinet.it<br>www.sirianrevelations.net

Or write:<br>Patricia Cori<br>Via Barberini 68<br>00187 Rome, Italy

# *Appendices*

## Move The Earth
### NASA's Answer to Global Warming:

Robin McKie–Science Editor
©The Guardian 10 June 2001

Scientists have found an unusual way to prevent our planet overheating: move it to a cooler spot. All you have to do is hurtle a few comets at Earth, and its orbit will be altered. Our world will then be sent spinning into a safer, colder part of the solar system. This startling idea of improving our interplanetary neighborhood is the brainchild of a group of NASA engineers and American astronomers who say their plan could add another six billion years to the useful lifetime of our planet–effectively doubling its working life.

"The technology is not at all far-fetched", said Dr Greg Laughlin, of the NASA Ames Research Center in California. "It involves the same techniques that people now suggest could be used to deflect asteroids or comets heading towards Earth. We don't need raw power to move Earth, we just require delicacy of planning and maneuvering" The plan put forward by Dr Laughlin, and his colleagues Don Korycansky and Fred Adams, involves carefully directing a comet or asteroid so that it sweeps close past our planet and transfers some of its gravitational energy to Earth. "Earth's orbital speed would increase as a result and we would move to a higher orbit away from the Sun", Laughlin said. Engineers would then direct their comet so that it passed close to Jupiter or Saturn, where the reverse process would occur. It would pick up energy from one of these giant planets. Later its orbit would bring it back to Earth, and the process would be repeated. In the short term, the plan provides an ideal solution to global warming, although the team was actually concerned with a more drastic danger. The Sun is destined to heat up in about a billion years and so "seriously compromise" our biosphere–by frying us. Hence the group's decision to try to save Earth. "All you have to do is strap a chemical rocket to an asteroid or comet and fire it at just the right time", added Laughlin. "It is basic rocket science."

The plan has one or two worrying aspects, however. For a start, space engineers would have to be very careful about how they directed their asteroid or comet towards Earth. The slightest miscalculation in orbit could fire it straight at Earth—with devastating consequences. It is a point acknowledged by the group. "The collision of a 100-kilometre diameter object with the Earth at cosmic velocity would sterilize the biosphere most effectively, at least to the level of bacteria", they state in a paper in *Astrophysics and Space Science*. "The danger cannot be overemphasized."

There is also the vexed question of the Moon. As the current issue of Scientific American points out, if Earth was pushed out of its current position it is "most likely the Moon would be stripped away from Earth", it states, radically upsetting out planet's climate. These criticisms are accepted by the scientists. "Our investigation has shown just how delicately Earth is poised within the solar system", Laughlin admitted. "Nevertheless, our work has practical implications. Our calculations show that to get Earth to a safer, distant orbit, it would have to pass through unstable zones and would need careful nurturing and nudging. Any alien astronomers observing our solar system would know that something odd had occurred, and would realize an intelligent life form was responsible." And the same goes for us.

When we look at other solar systems, and detect planets around other suns–which we are now beginning to do–we may see that planet-moving has occurred. It will give us our first evidence of the handiwork of extra-terrestrial beings.'

## Hint of Drifting Planet-Sized Drifters
## Bewilders Hubble Scientists
http://oposite.stsci.edu/pubinfo/PR/2001/20/pr.html
28 June 2001

Piercing the heart of a globular star cluster with its needle-sharp vision, NASA's Hubble Space Telescope has uncovered tantalizing clues to what could potentially be a strange and unexpected population of wandering, planet-sized objects.

In results published this week in *Nature*, the international science journal, Kailash Sahu (Space Telescope Science Institute, Baltimore, MD) and colleagues report six unusual microlensing events inside the globular cluster M22. Microlensing occurs when a background star brightens momentarily as a foreground object drifts by. The unusual objects thought to cause these events are far too dim to be seen directly, but instead were detected by the way their gravitational field amplifies light from a distant background star in the huge central bulge of our galaxy. Microlensing has been used before to search for low-mass objects in the disk and halo of our galaxy, but Hubble's sharp vision is essential to probe the interiors of globular clusters further.

From February 22 to June 15, 1999, Sahu and colleagues monitored 83,000 stars, detecting one clear microlensing event caused by a normal dwarf star in the cluster (about one tenth the mass of our Sun). As a result of gravitational lensing, the background star appeared to grow 10 times brighter and then returned to its normal brightness over a period of 18 days.

In addition to the microlensing event caused by the dwarf star, Sahu and his team recorded six even more interesting, unexpectedly brief events where a background star jumped in brightness by as much as a factor of two for less than 20 hours before dropping back to normal brightness. This means that the microlensing object must have been much smaller than a normal star.

These microlensing events were unusually brief, indicating that the mass of the intervening object could be as little as 80 times that of Earth. Objects this small have never before been detected by microlensing observations. If these results are confirmed by follow-up Hubble observations, the bodies would be the smallest celestial objects ever seen that are not orbiting any star.

So what are they? **Theoretically they might be planets that were gravitationally torn away from parent stars in the cluster.** However, they are estimated to make up as much as 10 percent of the cluster's mass—too numerous to be wandering, "orphaned" planets.

The results are so surprising, the astronomers caution that these preliminary observations must be confirmed by follow-up Hubble observations. If verified, these dark denizens could yield new insights about how stars and planets formed in the early universe. "Hubble's excellent sharpness allowed us to make this remarkable new type of observation, successfully demonstrating our ability to see very small objects," says Sahu. "This holds tremendous potential for further searches for dark, low-mass objects."

"Since we know that globular clusters like M22 are very old, this result opens new and exciting opportunities for the discovery and study of planet-like objects that formed in the early universe," adds co-investigator Nino Panagia (European Space Agency and Space Telescope Science Institute). "This initial observation shows that our microlensing method works beautifully," states co-investigator Mario Livio (Space Telescope Science Institute).

As microlensing events are brief, unpredictable and rare, astronomers improve their chances of observing one by looking at many stars at once—much like a person buying several lottery tickets at once. Most microlensing searches have been aimed at the central bulge of our galaxy or out towards the Magellanic Clouds—the densest observable regions of stars in the sky. In general these surveys cover areas of sky larger than the full Moon and look for foreground objects lying somewhere between us and the background population of stars.

Sahu and his team took advantage of Hubble's superb resolution and narrow field of view to aim the telescope directly through the center of a globular star cluster lying between Earth and the galactic bulge. This gave the team a very dense stellar region to probe for drifting low-mass foreground objects and a very rich background field of stars to be lensed. Only Hubble's resolution is sharp enough to actually peer through the crowded center of the cluster and see the far more distant stars in the galactic bulge. As the lensing objects were part of the cluster, the astronomers also had an accurate distance (8,500 light-years) and velocity for these objects.

In a normal lensing event, a background star brightens and dims for a length of time depending on the mass of the lensing body. The short, "spurious" events seen by the team are shorter than the interval between the Hubble observations, leading to an upper estimate for the mass of an object of one quarter Jupiter's mass.

To confirm these extraordinary, but tentative results, Sahu and colleagues next plan to monitor the center of the globular cluster continuously over a seven-day interval. They expect to detect 10 to 25 short-duration microlensing events, which will be well-sampled enough to yield direct measurements of the true masses of the small bodies.

This release is issued jointly by NASA *http://www.nasa.gov* and ESA *http://www.esrin.esa.it*

Report from
**Dr. Virgilio Sánchez-Ocejo**
Miami UFO Center
www. ufomiami.homestead.com/index.html
15 June 2001

According to reports obtained by Marcial Campos Maza, a reporter for Chile's EFE news service, Chilean troops captured three creatures (Chupacabras) in the desert near the Radomiro Tomic mine north of Calama, Chile. During the pursuit, a fire-fight ensued in which one Chilean soldier was reportedly killed. The three creatures—a male, a female and a baby—were held at the regiment's barracks for several hours. Then a NASA team reportedly arrived by helicopter to take custody of them.

Some residents of Calama, however, claimed that the Chupacabras were 'creations' of NASA. "The gringos had at least three genetic experiments run away from them, and they've only able to capture two of them" said Dagoberto Corante, a Chilean architect. Residents of Calama and nearby communities continued to blame NASA, the U.S. space agency, for the apparitions and attacks of the mysterious Chupacabras, which has killed farm animals in the region and in other parts of Chile.

According to Dagoberto Corante, one such creature was captured by elements of a local (army) regiment in an operation that resulted in the death of one soldier, but the (Chilean) military has allegedly refused to discuss the matter. "It was said that the captured animal was kept all day at the regiment's barracks until NASA experts arrived to take it away" said Corante, who is a well-known and respected in the area where the Chupacabras feasted on blood and spread fear among the population. "On the day that the event transpired, the military even closed the Calama airport for several hours to enable the landing of a helicopter conveying American scientists," he added, "although no one is quite sure why they would close an airport in order for a helicopter to function—those are devices to land anywhere, and the fact has given rise to much speculation."

When we visited Calama, in July of last year, we interviewed eye witnesses of the presence of American personal in the area. One of them, an official in the Chilean army, will retire at the end of this year and we hope he will move forward with his experience.

Mr. Vega also reported to me that when he discussed this case with his cousin, who works at the Calama airport, he learned that a NASA jet plane has been, for over a month, at the airport and he had helped unload cages and sophisticated equipment. In one incident, he helped cover it with a canvas covering. The following Sunday, the two went to the airport and Mr. Vega saw, under the canvas covering, the NASA logo on the wings and tail of a small passenger jet plane. These are only a few of eye witnesses testimonies we obtained in Calama, and that were not covered by the press. Mr. Juan Vega is the school Director of Colegio Ecologico Montessori, he has a master in Biology and Chemistry.

There has been a cover-up on the part of the authorities, until now, and Senator Carlos Cantero is asking, why? We hope that NASA involvement in that region will show up.

RUMOR: According to a local newspaper, La Estrella del Loa, Tuesday August 1, 2000, NASA used the Atacama Desert as a test ground for a vehicle in its Project Mars, it is believed they also left three genetic experiments (Chupacabras) as part of this project.

## Scientists Create GM Algae
## Which Grows Without Sunlight
©Reuters LT 2001
15 June 2001

WASHINGTON (Reuters)–Scientists said on Thursday they had genetically engineered a type of algae to grow without sunlight, a breakthrough that could cut the cost of growing the single-celled plant used in dietary supplements. The addition of a single gene caused the algae to give up sunlight as its primary energy source–a process known as photosynthesis–and use glucose, a sugar, instead, researchers said in a study appearing in the journal Science. Commercial cultivation of algae is typically done in large outdoor ponds, where contamination by microbes and variations in sunlight and temperature can reduce the quality and quantity of the plants, the scientists said. "Eliminating contamination means that the algae can be produced at a high purity for pharmaceutical applications or dietary supplements", said study co-author Kirk Apt of Martek Biosciences Corp.

In addition to dietary supplements such as beta-carotene and the fatty acid DHA, algae is used in fluorescent pigments for scientific labeling and in food for commercial fish farms. The scientists said they also found that the gene-altered algae grew at 15 times the density of sunlight-grown algae, partly because the algae in outdoor ponds can shade each other, restricting the available light. To get the algae called *Phaeodactylum tricornutum* to feed off glucose or another carbon compound instead of sunlight, a single gene from either human red blood cells or another type of algae was inserted, they said. These so-called glucose transporter genes changed the metabolism of the algae into glucose eaters, allowing them to grow in darkness. The scientists said future efforts to change the metabolism of plants through genetic engineering likely would be more complicated than just adding a single gene. P. tricornutum was primed for the change because it has the complete cellular pathway for breaking down glucose "preinstalled" and the additional gene simply allowed the plant to take advantage of its own biology, they said.

## Chemtrails: Taking A Stand
Diane Harvey
merak@sedona.net
24 June 2001

What is it that all of us involved in this pestiferous chemtrail issue have in common? It isn't just the wretched fact of being bombarded from above with sickening unknown substances, by unknown persons, for unknown reasons. We do seem to know something now, about what is being done to us and why. This is not comforting either, because chemtrails are just the tail of the technological dragon. What really brings us together is something much deeper even than this. And that is, that all of us see the disappearance, before our eyes, of all influence on our own future, and on the future of our children and grandchildren. On the surface, we are brought together by an investigation into what must be the most complex and expensive secret operation ever perpetrated on an unsuspecting population. So, beneath this outrageous monumental techno-crime, is the much larger specter of an absolutely out-of-control runaway government. 'They', whoever they are, are dragging us, wherever they are going, by force. We aren't being asked for our cooperation, or for our votes. This means that the very word 'government' is now effectively meaningless.

WHAT government? Where is it? Who is it? Can we say we know the first thing about who is in fact actually running our country? No. And this is what lies at the very bottom of all of our very justifiable fears. On any practical and meaningful level, we are no longer citizens of a Republic at all. The sham of our supposed leaders, pretending to conduct a free and democratic society in our name, is a despicable insult to our intelligence. This is a very terrible fact we are looking in the eye here. And it leads us directly to the other important part of the eerie historical moment we re living in. Which is that, not only do we have no idea who is making the decisions for us now, we don't even have a population that cares.

There is something frighteningly wrong with the American people right now. A mysterious fog has settled down over people's minds. Something beyond run-of-the-mill human apathy has overtaken this society. People have lost something so fundamental to human life that we can hardly believe it, even though we see its effects constantly. We can describe what we see, but we can barely grapple with the meaning of it. This is something new under the sun, and it is very strange. But it is real, and we know it. People are disconnected from basic reality at a level that actually seems impossible. The fact that our government has gone off without us into dark secret places is a great crisis for our nation. But if our country were populated by alert, responsible and indignant citizens, this would not be happening. "It is not the function of our government to keep the citizen from falling into error; it is the function of the citizen to keep the government from falling into error." [Justice Robert H. Jackson]

It has taken a long time to entirely sever so many human beings from their own consciences. It has taken decades of slow, careful, deliberate numbing on many fronts. To send most of a nation into a kind of life-long sleeping sickness of the mind has required methodical planning, and the enthusiastic cooperation of the people themselves. This peculiar condition of mass entrancement we are grappling with now was no accident. A hundred years ago it would not have been possible to radically alter the sky itself right under the noses of the public without them noticing. This basic point is extremely significant to our effort. We are trying to awaken people who, quite often and very decisively, do not want to know what is happening to them, or to their country. Most of our fellow citizens are literally in a self-induced trance state. They have actually unconsciously decided not to comprehend what they are seeing and hearing. They have renounced common sense, in order not to be disturbed. It takes a tremendous effort, intelligence, skillful timing and the right approach even to make a dent in this epidemic of willful ignorance.

There have been hidden influences acting behind the scenes in this country for a very long time. What we are looking at in our generation is the result in the present of a very long history of corruption and secret influences. The roots of the present evil are old and deep. Even in his day, Henry David Thoreau looked around very carefully and said: "How does it become a man to behave toward the American government today? I answer that he cannot without disgrace be associated with it." Far too soon after the glorious beginnings of our nation, the American people began to display a tendency to let things go on without their involvement, and in this we haven't been different from other people in other nations. Relatively few people have ever felt responsible for trying to fix what was wrong with the power structure of their time.

In essence, relatively few have ever wanted to understand or to undertake the responsibilities for human freedom. Self-government by any people has had a very short shelf life in human history so far, for reasons that are sadly obvious to us today. Thomas Paine understood this, when he warned: "Those who expect to reap the blessings of freedom must undergo the fatigue of supporting it". This history we are so habituated to, of a politically apathetic and disinterested population, has added up to a cost most people never foresaw. The price we have paid without noticing has become all too clear. Our country, as it lives in our imaginations, no longer has any existence in the real world. Unfortunately, the perennial themes of letting things go, generation after generation, has culminated in a government that has now entirely disappeared out from under us. Whatever and whoever it is, it is holed up somewhere out of sight.

We are left holding the bag of misdirection: empty words, empty gestures, and empty appearances. We are here because we have eyes that can still see, and ears that can still hear. We have hearts that are still open and minds that still think. And above all else, we still hear and obey the dictates of conscience. Each of us knows that this is nothing special, but merely living as we were created to live. But it becomes a very special way to live when the majority of our fellow beings renounce all responsibility for their own lives at the most dangerous moment in history. When so many other people refuse to see and hear and understand, then the

Accidental Activist is born. There isn't one of us who could ever have imagined spending so much time and energy this way. We are activists by default, because the majority of people have renounced their responsibilities as citizens. We become self-appointed voices of our national conscience because we have no other self-respecting choice. Each of us has accepted the single pertinent fact: If not me, then who?

When democracy actually exists, it is not necessary to have credentials or affiliates or titles other than that of concerned citizen. As Ralph Nader pointed out: "A couple of thousand years ago in Athens, a man could get up in the morning, wander around the city, and inquire into matters affecting his well-being and that of his fellow citizens. No one asked him 'Who are you with?'" Has the majority of our population always been unwilling to notice what is inconvenient to notice? Has the majority inevitably left it to the few to demand justice for all? We can see that it has, and in this way we are re-enacting an old pattern. But there are many worse aspects to our present predicament than those who lived before us had to contend with.

What we are obliged to tackle, merely by being aware of it at all, is the lethal combination of concealed power, secret technology and an unprecedented level of materialism that powerfully induces mass sleeping sickness. We have a de facto clandestine government, practicing without a license. The long arm of the military is growing in the dark, reaching out to affect every living thing on Earth without the slightest oversight or agreement from the profoundly affected. People have, on the whole, traded normal awareness for highly destructive substitutes, and the evidence of their senses for the short-lived comforts of being undisturbed by reality.

What is there then to hope for, in looking at so many kinds of dark forces arrayed against us? There are hopeful elements in this picture, despite appearances to the contrary. One great hope is in the fact that we have no leaders. Good government in our country has so far relied heavily on the existence of occasional great leaders. Since such people are always rare, in a very real sense this has been a serious weakness inherent in the practical working out of the democratic ideal. Great leaders have come and gone, but the citizenry, the supposed bedrock of a freedom-loving people, has not been sufficiently involved in national life. Yet things are so bad now that more and more people are being forced to realize that they have been tricked and abandoned by the wayside. We are not rare specimens, but part of a significant number of people who see things going disastrously off the rails in various ways. In every country human beings are looking around and wondering why they should put up with having no say at all in their own world.

We might be surprised at how many of us there are, still divided by different issues, yet united in the basic understanding of what we are looking at. But the price of such dedication to the original principles of active citizenship is extraordinarily high these days. When so many are so afraid to exercise their basic rights and duties, those who choose to do so are forced to pay dearly for their efforts in behalf of all. Simply by taking our own Constitution seriously, we make ourselves outcasts. "You need only reflect that one of the best ways to get yourself a reputation as a dangerous citizen these days is to go about repeating the very phrases which our founding fathers used in their struggle for independence." [Charles A. Beard] It is a hard business to endure being seen as a dangerous and tedious eccentric when you know you are merely awake. It is harder than we could have imagined, to spend so much time, energy and money trying to make up for what an entire nation ought to be doing along with us. And it is hardest of all to suffer, as many have, painful discord in relationships with family and friends.

What is more agonizing than being obliged on occasion to choose between truth and justice for all, and a comforting personal relationship? We do not romanticize the difficulties of serving a great cause- we have experienced the hardships far too acutely for that. But we have in common that what we know has swept up our personal hopes, wishes, and dreams into another and far larger field of life. We are living now in a larger world of extreme human necessity. Our source of nourishment is the spirit of freedom itself. Because what is slowly but surely coming into being, through all our efforts, is the renewal of the original energy that created this country in the first place. The deepest truth in all of this is that we are serving the sacred purposes of life itself at a critical and momentous time in human history. And for this opportunity, despite all our difficulties, and despite the forces arrayed against us, we are profoundly grateful.

*This speech by Diane Harvey was delivered through the kind auspices of David Peterson, at Wright Patterson Air Force Base, on June 23, 2001.*

# Glossary of Terms

Akashic Record:      Etheric memory of all time, place and consciousness of the universe, which exists in the DNA of all conscious beings.

Alchemy:      The refinement of matter; the transmutation of physical 'laws'.

Annunaki:      The ruling elite of the planet Nebiru, a three-dimensional planet which travels between the Sirius system and our solar system in a 3,600 year orbit.

Ascension:      The soul's journey from darkness to light.

Astral journeying:      The separation of the astral body from the physical body, during which time one experiences other dimensions, states of consciousness and realities.

Atlán:      The capital of Atlantis—cultural, scientific and spiritual center of the Atlantean civilization, specifically referring to the 3rd cycle.

Chakras:      The main energy vortices of the body, points where the Ida and Pingala energy byways intersect.

Chupacabras:      An animal 'unlike anything known on Earth' which has been terrorizing people, attacking cattle and animals in Puerto Rico and in Chile, result of genetic experiments in the underground.

Crop circles:      Geometrical configurations appearing mysteriously in crop fields at various points of the world (particularly in the southern region of England)–connection points for extraterrestrial intelligence and Earth energies.

*Desert Days:* The period of desertification and violent environmental changes which precede planetary ascension.

*Earth Changes:* Earth's mental, emotional and physical response to global and universal events.

*Gaia:* Earth, the conscious being, a multidimensional deity.

*Golden Mean:* Pythagoras's measure of the divine geometry, manifest in the biological forms of Earth.

*Great Experiment:* The seeding of Planet Earth with the genetic material of alien species for the creation of the super race, Homo Sapiens.

*Grid:* The electromagnetic force field that was placed around the Earth at the time of the seeding of Homo Sapiens–used to scramble the frequencies coming in from the Family of Light and hold the race in servitude.

*HAARP:* High Frequency Active Aural Research Project–secretive military 'research' project designed to beam two billion watts of radiated power into the ionosphere.

*Suggested reading:* *Angels Don't Play this Haarp, Jeanne Manning & Dr. Nick Begich–Earthquake Press.*

*Hyperdimensional Spiral:* The Julia Set crop circle configuration, which appeared across the road from the Stonehenge monument, July 1966.

*Karma:* Cause and effect; the creation and result of actions and thoughts that are carried forward as the soul journeys the spiral.

| | |
|---|---|
| *Light:* | Knowledge and love. |
| *Mindlight generators:* | A network of crystal generators, activated by the collective mind power of the citizenry, in the Last Generation of Atlantis. |
| *Multidimensional:* | Comprised of many dimensions, from the dense to the refined, existing as vibrational frequencies. |
| *Neteru:* | Egyptian term for 'gods'; the Speakers assert that it is derived from the word, Nebiru. |
| *Orichalcum:* | A highly conductive metal ore that was abundantly available in Atlantis and which was utilized for storage of energy, healing and building. |
| *Poseidon Chromodome:* | The great healing temple located in Atlán. Among the most important cures were color baths, crystal energy re-balancing and swimming with the Dolphin Beings. |
| *Power Points:* | Key energy vortices of Gaia, similar to the chakras of human beings. |
| *Resonance:* | The reaching of a common wavelength of varying vibrational frequencies. |
| *Retrogradation:* | The appearance of going backward or regressing while actually moving forward; returning to the physical reality from higher states of consciousness, of crystallizing back into matter. |
| *Secret Government:* | Three-dimensional individuals of Annunaki lineage who are directed by the Annunaki in the management of the Earth. |
| *Selenite tuning rods:* | Crystalline 'tuning' forks used by the Atlantean Priestesses to tune the musical patterns of the |

|                       |                                                                                                                                                        |
| --------------------- | ------------------------------------------------------------------------------------------------------------------------------------------------------ |
|                       | body, much as one tunes a piano by with a tuning fork.                                                                                                   |
| *Starseed:*           | Non-indigenous life forms on any given planet body.                                                                                                      |
| *Temple of Nephthys:* | The amethyst temple of the Yzhnüni. Here was found the Temple of the Skulls, the thirteen crystal skulls of Atlantis.                                     |
| *Wam:*                | The primordial chord; the music of the soul.                                                                                                             |
| *Yod:*                | The basic sacred form of the Hebrew alphabet, understood to hold the key to understanding of the Kaballah.                                               |
| *Yzhnüni:*            | The first Sirian light beings to crystallize in Atlantis.                                                                                                |

# Index

Printed in the United Kingdom
by Lightning Source UK Ltd.
121174UK00001BA/25-27